I'm a
Stranger
Here Myself

I'm a Stranger Here Myself

JOAN SCOBEY

St. Martin's/Marek
New York

Design by Lee Wade

Library of Congress Cataloging in Publication Data
Scobey, Joan.
    I'm a stranger here myself.
    1. Middle age—United States. I. Title.
HQ1059.5.U5S26 1984   305.2′44′0973   83-23117
ISBN 0-312-35673-0

First Edition
10 9 8 7 6 5 4 3 2 1

To my parents and my children, who unintentionally taught me about middle age, and to Rafe, who is a faster learner than I am.

CONTENTS

I'm a
Stranger
Here Myself

I'M A
STRANGER
HERE MYSELF

You're always too young for it.

It usually takes you by surprise.

It's never welcome.

The topic is middle age.

Small comfort that the condition is epidemic. Or that by the time you realize there is absolutely nothing you can do about it, you find it's not as bad as you feared. Or that, as you observe those ahead of you struggling with this unwelcome passage, most people eventually seem to make the best of it.

It's still middle age.

Its symptoms can be acute or chronic. Acute is the sudden and painful awareness of your own mortality: You (or a contemporary) are stricken by serious illness. Your remaining parent dies. Your youngest child leaves home. Chronic are the unexpected telltales that flag the passage of time: You take your nephew to lunch and pick up the check, then take your mother to lunch and pick up the check. You realize, when *The Postman Always Rings Twice* comes to your neighborhood theater, that you saw the original version. You still associate the Dodgers with Brooklyn and Tuesday night television with Milton Berle. Accumulated reminders, each conveniently repressed until something triggers the shock of recognition: *Middle age! Me?*

The catalyst for my own mid-life confrontation was benign—an invitation to my thirtieth college reunion—but it did the job. It forced a compelling question: How can I still feel twenty-seven—actually believe in my head I am twenty-seven—if my classmates are fifty-one? The invitation to the twenty-fifth reunion triggered no similar response; I had no doubt then that I was twenty-seven and no symptoms, acute or chronic, suggested otherwise. In the intervening five years, however, our children had taken up permanent residence elsewhere and we were no longer live-in parents, two close friends had died, life-threatening illness had assaulted friend and family, and, to be frank, it now takes a hot shower every morning to get the joints moving. But even in the face of accumulating evidence, I am unwilling to acknowledge a twenty-eighth birthday —not, at least, without investigation. An opportunity seemed at hand.

"Say," I propose to my classmate Rosa, "let's go to the local pre-reunion lunch and see how everyone is doing."

Over the sherry we discover that most of our classmates are doing fine, but all too many of them resemble cheerful grandmothers. Gray hair, white hair, laugh lines, crow's-feet, wrinkles, chins.

"Do we look like that?" I whisper to Rosa.

"No, no," she assures me. "Not at all like that."

And in my eagerness to believe her, it doesn't occur to me that our classmates might be saying the same thing about us.

Disbelief that somehow we have involuntarily stumbled into this dreaded time of life doesn't dull our appetite to find out what it's all about. We need to define ourselves, know where we stand. This particular passage makes us nervous, perhaps because we aren't quite sure what lies ahead. As psychologist Daniel Levinson wrote in *The Seasons of a Man's Life*, "Adults hope that life begins at 40—but the great anxiety is that it ends there."*

My own anxiety is not that life ends at middle age (that might be preferable to what I was beginning to fear), but that inevitably it will be downhill from now on. Despite still feeling twenty-seven, is the best behind me or do new pleasures still lie ahead? Am I at the beginning or the end of the line? And if I am somewhere in transit, what will make this leg of the trip worthwhile? What, in fact, is middle age anyway?

The answers must lie with my perplexed contemporaries, like me caught by surprise in the middle, no longer young but not yet old. By taking a half-time pause, questioning colleagues, observing

*Notes to chapters begin on page 142

friends, consulting experts in adult development, perhaps we can make sense of this paradoxical time of life.

Most of my respondents are married. Most of them have children. They are thus provided with (usually) graying spouses and (invariably) growing offspring to remind them of time's passing. But they don't have an exclusive on the panics and pleasures that seem to strike universally at mid-life without regard to family status.

Note: One possible flaw in my sociological study is that I am both observer and participant; I decided arbitrarily that being an interested player might be unscientific but not disadvantageous. I spend my time with the precise population under scrutiny. I witness (and usually share) the mid-life madness brought on by the shocking recognition: Middle age? Us? Moreover, I don't have any preconceived notions of what middle age really is. After all, I'm a stranger here myself.

The first thing I discovered is that there is increasing interest in this middle generation. Perhaps because so many of us are getting older—in the next decade a third of the country will be over forty-five—people are paying attention to us. Magazines that formerly addressed a readership strictly between eighteen and thirty-four now occasionally speak to a mid-life population. Social scientists now study us (often prompted to take our middle-aged temperatures by a precipitous elevation in their own fever charts as they enter their middle years).

The next thing I noticed was that as soon as we fear we are nudging middle age, the subject becomes all-engrossing. What has heretofore been rejected or ignored is now of prime concern. Like all those dreary tales other people tell of their back problems, sciatic spasms, musculature gone awry . . . BORING. That is, until you bend over to tie your sneakers and can't get up . . . and can't stop telling everyone how absolutely unique and terrible the pain is.

That's how middle age hits people. It's a topic of no interest—until you are the topic. Then most people can't keep their minds off it. They talk about it constantly, sometimes just to deny it. They read about it voraciously, hoping for optimistic reports. They tarry at newsstands brazenly thumbing through magazines that headline, "It Isn't Fun Till You're Forty" or "Sophia Loren [Angie Dickinson, Mary Tyler Moore, Jane Fonda], Mid-life Marvel!" They stitch lighthearted sayings to ease the pain: "After forty, it's patch, patch, patch" . . . "If you are pushing fifty, that's exercise enough."

We are bewildered by the paradoxes that mark the territory. At times we feel younger than our children, older than our parents, and often generally undefinable—sometimes all at the same time. Moreover, as sharp an eye as we keep on our own aging, monitoring each wrinkle and stray gray hair, we are likely to spot the first signs of middle age in someone else, a friend, a classmate, or someone even closer to home—a spouse.

Small wonder we can't get a fix on it. Middle age is a completely subjective concept, an amorphous state that appears one way to young people, another to old people, and may not exist at all in the minds of those in between. Its limits defy definition. Our children seem to mature earlier, assuming their places in the adult world at ever younger ages; our parents seem to stay younger longer—or at least to begin a conventional old age later. Twenty-six year olds head high-tech companies; grandmothers fly planes. And in between, the rest of us are doing the same things for a longer time, or are stretching our middle years with second careers, second families, second lives that are often radically different from our first. "Since there are no clear boundaries," observes Bernice L. Neugarten, professor of education and sociology at Northwestern University, "it is sometimes said that middle age should be described as a state of mind rather than as a given period of years."

Nevertheless, people try to categorize it. Pin it down. Define precisely when it begins and how long it lasts. But virtually the only constant about middle age is the number 40. Somewhere around age forty, even before some unexpected event has undeniably connected us to middle age, the idea of middle age first occurs to us —if only to reject it. For instance, one day when Tom Brokaw had just entered his forties, he introduced his television audience to "three young senators." He looked at the camera and smiled. "I say 'young' because they are roughly the same age as I am."

At the high end of this ill-defined generation is my eighty-two-year-old mother.

"Hey, Ma," I recently asked her. "When do you think middle age is?"

4

"I'll let you know when I get there."

Social scientists are no more successful in their efforts to quantify middle age. Analyzing one study on human development at the University of Chicago, Neugarten reports: "Among business executives and professionals, a man did not reach middle age until 50, nor old age until 70. For the blue-collar worker, on the other hand, life was paced more rapidly, and a man was described as middle-aged by 40 and old by 60."

To further muddy the demographics, when my friend Carol was thirty, she heard a woman of sixty-four call herself middle-aged. Her eyes popped. Now she is a social worker and close to sixty-four herself. She recently interviewed a woman in her mid-fifties.

"Are there any particular stresses you're finding in middle age?" she asked the patient.

"Middle age? Who's middle-aged?"

"Ummm," said Carol in her most nonjudgmental manner. "What would you consider middle age?"

"Well," said the patient, "I guess it's about ten years from now."

The fact that in ten years she will be eligible for Social Security doesn't change the reality of the observation. Nobody seems to have any better definition. Like a herd of wildebeest parting in front of an advancing Land Rover, middle age keeps a well-defined and inviolate space between it and the advancing subject. It simply depends on who you are and where you're standing.

All the old social rules have changed, and they profoundly affect the way we feel about ourselves in the middle years. When old as well as young couples are comfortable living together without benefit of the law, they recapture an unexpected sense of new beginnings. When men can risk second careers without being regarded as unstable or as failures, they gain a heightened sense of vitality. When women can shape second lives in productive work, they establish an exhilarating sense of self along with their independence and autonomy. We feel so young, so full of promise and vigor. How can this be middle age?

Even our vocabulary is changing. What used to be called middle age is frequently known now as mid-life. That has nice reverberations. It suggests activity, excitement, that we are where the action is, in the middle of liveliness. It trades the pejorative *middle age* for the optimistic *mid-life*. Swaps age for life. That's not a bad place to begin this investigation.

What follows is a report at halftime.

2

"YOU CAN'T BE ANNIE FOREVER"

Middle age is hard to pin down and understand not only because most people want to avoid it. They genuinely think of themselves as younger. Ask anyone. Most of us have an interior age, a magic time when the mind's clock stops ticking, allowing us to embrace health and vigor and wit for the rest of our days. As Satchel Paige, the baseball player, once said, "How old would you be if you didn't know how old you wuz?"

As I mentioned, I happen to be twenty-seven. Oh, if you ask me how old I am, I will reluctantly mumble, "Forty-two," or "forty-seven," or "fifty-three"—depending on when you asked me—or, more likely, "God, I'm fifty-three!" (Political songwriter Tom Lehrer, who also doesn't like the sound of fifty-three, prefers to say he is "eleven Celsius.") But ask me how old I am in my head and it's always twenty-seven. I don't know why it's always twenty-seven. Perhaps because it was after I was married and just before we had children, a romantic golden moment when everything was a beginning.

For a long time I thought it was an embarrassing but harmless vanity to think of myself as everlastingly twenty-seven. The day I confessed this to a friend I discovered I wasn't alone. "Of course! My magic age is twenty-three." (As long as I've known her, she has hated being several years older than me.) Why twenty-three? She isn't quite sure, but she feels it has something to do with that being the year she got married. That is, it was the year in which she was both single *and* married.

"I think I must have peaked then," she says. "I was probably performing at top efficiency at my job, and then I got married—and in those days, that kind of validated the success of one's life. Yes, it certainly was a good year."

My friend Judith puts her magic age at twenty-three, the year she graduated from law school.

"It was a professional triumph?" I suggest.

"No, it had nothing to do with career," she answers. "From that time on I've felt exactly the same in my head. I can't bear the thought that I'm forty-eight—the sense of fun and amusement with life and adventure is still exactly the same as when I was twenty-one."

Twenty-one is also the magic age of a fifty-year-old editor I know. "It was my first year of adulthood. A significant year. I could vote. I could drink. It was the first time I felt grown up, independent."

The same sense of feeling adult prompts pal Stella to place her magic age at thirty. Were there any special traumas or events? "No, nothing special happened. I just woke up one day and felt grown up. All of a sudden I no longer felt shy. I felt I could cope with things. I realized I knew more than many people about certain things— about how people behave, and why. And it's gotten better ever since."

Stella, I think, may have put her finger on it. That wonderful magic age may mark the first time we feel really good about ourselves, may signal a more-than-tenuous hold on a sense of identity. It may celebrate the joyous optimism we feel when we sense new beginnings while at the same time we first feel competent.

Does everyone, no matter his or her chronological age, place the magic age generally in the twenties, I wonder? So I ask my favorite senior respondent, my mother, how old she thinks she is.

"When I'm not having a cold," she sniffles, "I think I'm fifty. I really run around like a fifty year old. Of course, when I was fifty, I thought that was awfully old."

"Fifty? You really think in your head that you're fifty?"

"Well, to tell you the truth, Joan, it's really a lot younger, but I didn't want to shock you."

Lest you think it's only the folks I know who stake their claims to being younger, let me offer as evidence the results of a 1982 nationwide survey of 1,000 men and women. Four out of five of the respondents between forty and sixty perceived themselves an average of fifteen years younger (many felt twenty years younger). And as they got older, the difference between their chronological and perceived ages increased.

As George Bernard Shaw reminds us in *Man and Superman,* old age is not tolerated any better on earth than it is in hell by Don Juan, and that is one reason why in middle age—which we perceive as old —we seek more youthful times. But why the twenties or early thirties? Carol Froehlich, a psychiatric social worker who sees more than her share of mid-life problems, thinks we fix on an age when we had few responsibilities, a time of affirmation of ourselves, a time between the traumas of adolescence and the coming decisions about our life's work and marriage. Levinson ties it to our new and disheartening perception of the fragility of life. He writes, "At mid-life, the growing recognition of mortality collides with the powerful wish for immortality and the many illusions that help to maintain it." Surely our "magic age" is one of those illusions.

One reason it's possible to perpetuate this fantasy is that after we're thirty, for twenty or more years we look and act the same. We play the same sports at essentially the same level of skill; we may even attempt new ventures and perform creditably. We wear the same kinds of clothes, often in the same size (if not smaller). We exercise and take care of our bodies; many of us are trimmer and fitter now than we were twenty years earlier. Some of us so easily pass for our twenty-year-old daughters that the ads challenging us to tell which-is-the-mother don't surprise us.

Another reason it's possible to remain mentally in one's twenties or thirties is that for so many years after we leave them chronologically, we are in the company of our elders. Your boss is older. Your doctor. Your lawyer. Even your dentist is older.

At the same time, if you have children, for at least seventeen or eighteen years you are part of a vast parent population. No matter what your actual age, when you are all listening to the sixth grade teacher explain the binary system, you don't recognize age differences between the child-bride who is now thirty-one and the late-bearing mother who may be over fifty (at least not if you're the fifty year old). After all, you think, we both have twelve year olds. I must still be thirty-one, too.

From the time our first-born entered kindergarten and our last-born left high school, there was a span of sixteen years during which we shared the PTA and class plays with parents often twenty years younger (and older) than ourselves. I felt we were all contemporaries. It was one of the fringe benefits of paying your PTA dues. And we have only two children. Think of the extended youth that parents of larger families enjoy. They get to be thirty-one for eighteen, even twenty or more years.

This fantasy of extended youth is not the self-delusion it may first appear. The concept has its scientific basis. In a study of 2,000 people conducted at the University of Chicago, Neugarten found that the middle-aged don't define their age chronologically. "Middle-aged people look to their positions within different life contexts —body, career, family—rather than to chronological age for their primary cues in clocking themselves," she reports. Young children, a successful career, a trim and healthy body, all help us feel younger than our chronological age. Levinson is even more precise. He believes that when people are sharing similar experiences, they tend to regard anyone who is six or seven years younger or older than themselves as roughly the same age.

Whether you have felt yourself a thirty-one-year-old elementary school parent for twelve or twenty years, one day you find yourself older than everybody else. It occurs with startling suddenness. It may happen when you realize that the nice young doctor who is helping your regular pediatrician has become your regular pediatrician. Or when your children complain of sharing his office waiting room with infants in bulky snowsuits and want a "real doctor." Moreover, they are not satisfied with the gray-haired father figure who treats you; they want a younger guy who will ask *them* if they need any contraceptive information.

Our family happens to have a gray-haired family doctor who readily dispenses contraceptive information, and even excludes protective mothers from his gynecological consultations with their daughters, so my initial brush with "ageism" came from another direction.

The first time I realized I was gaining on the father figures of my life was during the Kennedy administration. John F. Kennedy was forty-three when he was inaugurated, and more than ten years older than I. My generation was accustomed to looking up to people in authority. We accepted them as older, wiser, more mature. We followed their advice and direction. We were the ones who never removed the Do-Not-Remove-This-Tag-Under-Penalty-Of-Law label from our living room pillows. So when JFK said, "Ask not what your country can do for you; ask what you can do for your country," I asked. I wanted very much to do something for my country. For anyone—as long as I was home by noon to feed David and Ricky lunch. Here, leading our country, was an administration that valued vigor and energy. Here, from nine to twelve, was this young mother full of vigor and energy. It was not that I expected to be a White House Scholar; it was simply that the rhythms of my life, my generation, seemed nicely in sync with the larger world.

JFK, however, was staffing his administration with *youths* of vim and vigah. The senior citizens of Camelot turned out to be thirty-two. LBJ, perhaps the quintessential federal father figure, was older —but much of his staff was even younger. And here were my peers and I getting a little older, much wiser, and even better prepared to contribute to the Great Society—and all of a sudden we were too old for it. On Monday still young, a lifetime of public service ahead of us. On Tuesday, over the hill. The fashion seemed to change overnight.

"Hey," I said. "It's still me—only a day older."

"Too bad," said They. "The job descriptions specify age twenty-six to thirty-five."

It was not literally true, of course, that a person over thirty-five couldn't find employment. But the perception persisted among employers that, nearing forty, you had peaked and were sliding. Past your prime. Useful, perhaps even beloved, to family and friends. To an employer maybe even choice quality, but no longer prime.

I don't know if others felt this as keenly as I did. It seemed to me that our whole generation was co-opted, preempted. It was as if, just as we were all getting our acts together, the curtain came down on the finale.

By the time Richard Nixon came around and began to bring back the middle age I was used to seeing in high office, it occurred to me that fairly soon the President himself was going to be younger

11

than I. Or, to put it in the perspective that actually occurred to me: I was going to be older than the President. I don't like being older than anybody, and especially not the Head of State. I sometimes suspect that I am not alone, and that is one reason—perhaps the main reason—why Ronald Reagan at age sixty-nine was elected President. He made age respectable. Suddenly the generation that was too old for Camelot was now wise, not wizened; mature, not overripe; ablaze, not burned out. Whatever else Ronald Reagan stood for, he represented the youthful hopes of an aging population voting for someone older than themselves.

It's not a bad idea. To paraphrase Senator Roman Hruska, who was defending the appointment of a mediocre judge to the Supreme Court, there are a lot of aging people, and they deserve representation, too.

"Sudden aging," it turns out, is a common syndrome around forty, familiar to the psychologists and social scientists who chart our developmental course. It simply happens to different people in different ways. Sometimes it's the creeping realization that more of your colleagues seem younger than you, the flight of stairs steeper, the newsprint smaller. Family events are the bell ringers for women, but not men, Neugarten found. "For married women, middle age is closely tied to the launching of children into the adult world, and even unmarried career women often discuss middle age in terms of the family they might have had."

On the other hand, Neugarten discovered that most men are notified of their advancing years outside the home, particularly at work. It might be the gradual change from bright young comer in the department to mentor, nurturing the next generation of bright young comers. Or a well-mannered associate who prefaces a question with "Sir," and ushers you through the door first. One man I know was shaken to his tasseled loafers when a polite young subway rider got up and offered him his seat.

Often it's a single dramatic event that illuminates the fragility of life. For many men it is the death by heart attack of a friend. For many women it's a mastectomy—and it needn't be a friend. Any contemporary will do. For myself, I knew for the first time that life wasn't forever when my husband and my father went to the hospital on the same day. Intimations of mortality abound, from the trivial discoveries of yet more wrinkles and gray hairs to the death of one's remaining parent. And in between, any decline or fall of whatever we value—our health, our bodies, our work, our family relationships.

Whatever the catalyst, the cause is our desperate wish for immortality. That is Levinson's view, and I believe him. "A man's fear that he is not immortal is expressed in his preoccupation with bodily decline and his fantasies of imminent death. The decline is normally quite moderate," he states, "but it is often experienced as catastrophic. A man fears that he will soon lose all the youthful qualities that make life worthwhile. Young is immortal, Old is the brink of death."

What Levinson calls the "Young/Old polarity" fosters a lot of fantasies. Sometimes mid-life men really do change their lives, their wives, their careers; sometimes they simply live on their fantasies. I know more than one mid-life man, for instance, who flies a plane not necessarily to get from here to there but because there is no honorable war that will let a middle-age pilot reclaim his youth. I see many men—and not a few women—who live out their dreams in sports cars and announce their desires on license plates: FEELSOGD . . . WICKED . . . SLY FOX . . . SHYSTER . . . BIGJIM . . . IMKEPT . . . FOOTZ . . . MS BABE. And for other fantasists who choose not to license their libidinous longings, the last convertible is back. Detroit may think of the convertible as a teen-age joy car; it is the middle-aged who need—and often buy—it.

The quest for youth/immortality also drives us to some crazy behavior. Our frantic attempts to back away from the brink sometimes catapult us backward into our children. The generations collide. It often seems as if we are trying to replace our adolescents with our own adolescence. Take our absorption with ourselves and our identity. The preoccupation with our bodies, our hair, our clothes. The mothers who dress younger than their daughters. The fathers with the turtlenecks, cowboy boots, blue jeans, the talismanic gold chains with their magical property of youth.

Expressive adornment may have reached its zenith with Lenny, a fifty-two-year-old real estate entrepreneur who sports gold-highlighted ringlets where before there were straight graying—and thinning—locks.

"A permanent!" exclaimed his cousin who ran into him at a family wedding.

"Look," said Lenny, "it hides the thin spots in the hair and, you know, makes you look younger."

"You're probably wearing chains under that tuxedo," said the cousin accusingly.

"Yeah," admitted Lenny, smiling sheepishly at his androgynous appearance. "The other night I woke up, felt my permanent, felt my chain necklace, felt my gold bracelet that spells out L-E-N, and I thought, When am I going to get my monthly period?"

Len's mod masquerade illustrates Levinson's view that we take our cues of young and old from cultural symbols—in Len's case from the hip swingers of popular entertainment. Len, like the rest of us, is just doing his best to stem the tide. As Levinson writes with sympathetic understanding, "It is hard to integrate the Young/Old polarity in the self when the external world draws such a hard line between young and old and makes it so frightening to be other than young."

It is probably just as frightening for our young when we move in on their territory. At least they are apt to be just as provoked and embarrassed by our behavior as we often are by theirs. Author and artist Tom Wolfe catches the essence of the young/old polarity in a cartoon in his book *In Our Time* called "The Generation Gap." It is Parents Day. The grade-school youngster is in Mary Janes, double-breasted velvet-collared melton coat, and cap. Her mother, with Farrah Fawcett tresses, is in sunglasses, bulky turtleneck over tights, long scarf flying. The child pulls her mother along the school path and says, "Puh-leeze, Mummy, nobody wants to hear about coke, Acapulco, or Fleetwood Mac."

We didn't need the child to remark on the emperor's new clothes to know that the clearest vision is often in the eye of young beholders—but that didn't persuade the king to change his attire. As one of the girls who played the title role of Annie sagely observed when she was fourteen and fast outgrowing her part, "You can't be Annie forever."

A lot of us are giving it a try.

3

LETTING GO

Most people don't need to measure themselves against the leader of the free world to realize that the meter is ticking. They have their first brush with aging on a beachhead closer to home. For many it's a high school graduation that hits like a riptide, flinging you rudely fast/forward. We had that one ourselves.

The day after our younger son's graduation from high school, a neighbor said to me, *"All* your children are out of school? Oh."

I hesitated to look in the mirror lest, like Dorian Gray, the exterior manifestation of old age was indeed as visible to others as the interior one suddenly seemed to me. That high school graduation was at least as traumatic in the lives of the parents as it was to the participant, and I have often thought the occasion would be marked more appropriately if graduation speakers addressed their you-are-entering-a-brave-new-era remarks to the parents instead of to the graduates.

I don't know why we should be so surprised at the pain of the separation or by the suddenness with which it strikes. Perhaps it is because we are still struggling so hard to separate our middle-aged selves from our own parents that we forget our rear flank is exposed. While trying to free ourselves from the generation ahead, we are of course the objects of the same liberation by the generation behind. An added irony is that we've been preparing for it for years—if only we had realized it. As my friend Laurie once remarked, "The thing about being a parent is that you're always saying good-bye. They never told us that."

The trouble is that some separations aren't clearly designated. Oh, I could tell that the first good-bye was at nursery school. "So long," I said. "Have a good time." And the next good-bye was clearly recognizable a few summers later when the camp train pulled out. But then there was a rainy day when David was in fourth grade. I didn't realize for many years that was also preparation for separation.

I was driving the car pool when I was treated to the results of a quiz given by the teacher of most of the car's occupants. The question was: If you could take three people with you to a desert island, whom would you take?

The first child to enter the car was crying because, after naming her parents, she had to choose between her brother and sister. "I had to leave one of them behind," she sobbed.

The second child had no trouble at all. She was a twin, the youngest of five children, and wise in survival tactics. She turned to her twin brother (who was not part of the quiz) and announced that she would take her other three siblings. The twin brother started to cry.

After we dropped the last child off, I said to David, "Lucky you didn't have a problem with the desert island." There are only four in our family all together.

"No problem," he said. "I told them I'd take Daddy, Ricky, and Ralph Sinsheimer."

Along the road to separating, children's bids for autonomy take many courses. Most of them are no surprise to their beleaguered parents; in fact, they are usually banal and predictable: the blasting music, the hair, the clothing—all styled to the trend of the moment, from rock to reggae, from patched (or unpatched) jeans to bawdy T-shirts announcing, say, A CENTURY OF WOMEN ON TOP—and always the umbilical telephone cord trailing into the bedroom, linking the adolescent fetus to an unseen organism. Some children seem to have taken a vow never to eat dinner with their parents; others demand such esoteric fare that their families only wish they would eat elsewhere. Jimmy was one kid who covered all the bases in sticking it to his parents. He had long disheveled hair, a very specific vegetarian diet that was lacto but not ovo, and a lust for a particular type of hand-fashioned leather sandals that cost more than his father's tasseled loafers. He was glad to eat dinner with his folks, at home or at any restaurant of their choice, even wear a tie and jacket if they so desired—as long as they understood he would be eating vegetarian and wearing the sandals.

David's declaration of independence was small and quiet. (Ricky's was large and resolute, but more of that later.) No sullen spells, no overt hostility. Only that wire coat hanger that for three months hung around his neck like a huge rigid triangular neckband. It performed its purpose of aggravating his father to distraction. Every night the old man came home from the office, sat down to dinner, and David would appear, hands washed, in clean (if ink-stained) blue jeans, with that wire hanger encircling his neck.

"David, do you really have to wear that to dinner?"

"Yes, Father."

Father never learned to ignore the hanger, which, of course, was the point of it all. It seemed to me a quintessentially David rebellion: It annoyed his father, it was perfectly harmless, and it certainly was original. David may have regarded it as a symbolic yoke, his link to the oppressed people of the world, or he may simply have wanted to feel closer to the tailor. In any case, eventually he tired of the wire noose and put it away. Perhaps he looked just as silly to himself as he did to us. Or, who knows, he may even have used it to hang up a piece of clothing. But one day he came to dinner, the same messy but polite child, *sans* hanger. And Pops had the grace not to comment.

Realizing in retrospect that the hanger was another episode in the long slow process of cutting loose from the parental fold, I recently asked David if there were other adolescent revolts we didn't catch.

"Just a little hash and pot at fifteen," he answered. "And the time you wouldn't let me go to the midnight concert of the Grateful Dead and I told you I was sleeping over at Henry's."

"You went to that concert?"

"Yes. We went to the midnight show, and we stayed for the three A.M. show, too. I told you I was sleeping over at Henry's, and I was."

There is no mistaking the good-bye at the Pan Am arrivals building when David comes home after three years in England. For one thing, I thought I was saying hello. He instructed me to meet his friend Denise at the airport. (I had already met Denise at Oxford, where she was one of the gang in the Sunday afternoon university touch football game. Denise was the girl jock with the sturdy throwing arm. Now she is The Lover.) So we recognize each other, and wait in the arrivals lounge. The sky darkens, a thunderstorm is brewing. Planes are being diverted to Hartford, Boston, Philadelphia, Washington. And still we wait, making polite talk. Does she like her new job? Is she settled in an apartment? How does the United States look to her after her years away? Every fifteen minutes we check the electronic arrivals board. After two hours, London Flight 101 is sent on to Hartford.

"I wouldn't do this for anyone else," says Denise. She smiles shyly, glimmers of eager anticipation in the large brown eyes. "Oh, this is so frustrating!"

We get coffee and an apple at the snack bar, and sit at the window, watching many planes take off. Nothing is landing. Aircraft activity at a major terminal always seems capricious, never more so than now. We move into the dark arrivals area. We have exhausted our conversation. The connecting link between us is sitting on an airstrip in Connecticut. I take out my paperback. She takes out hers.

Two more hours. Planes are starting to land. And finally Flight 101 is scheduled to arrive . . . in ten minutes. Denise can't believe it. She joins the throngs waiting along the arrivals corridor.

"What flight are you on?" she asks several passengers as they come through. I sit at a discreet distance, hanging onto my paperback.

"Mrs. Scobey," she says, "why don't you take a turn waiting now?"

"That's okay, Denise," I say.

"No," she says. "Your turn."

So I stand among the crowd peering into the customs area, scanning the arriving passengers each time the doors open. Ah! I spot the bearded son, almost ready to exit.

"Denise," I call to her, "here he comes."

Instinct tells me to retreat. I don't need to. The beard passes me by, drops the two suitcases, the tennis gear, the backpack, and envelops the girlfriend. They abandon the luggage and step out of the area altogether. Minutes later they emerge.

"Oh, hi, Mom. Thanks for coming to the airport."

For three years we have been anticipating a family reunion on home ground. The favorite chocolate roll was lovingly made. Wine is chilling. A flowering plant in full bloom is on his night table. All awaits the homecoming prince.

Hi, Mom. Thanks for coming to the airport.

It's almost midnight before we are finally home, through crawling traffic jammed by the weather, by road repairs, by irritable motorists.

"Look," says Rick, hugging his brother on his arrival home. "Dad brought Denise a half-dozen roses."

"Only five of them are for Denise," says the old man. "One is for Mom."

Learning to separate is a long slow process for both parties, and I wonder if we, on the senior side of the equation, did our part as readily as we might have. Actually, I know damn well we didn't; most of the time we didn't even know what to do. On this point I get some reassurance from psychoanalyst Roger L. Gould, M.D. "One moment we act toward our growing adolescent children as our parents acted toward us," he writes in *Transformations.* "The next moment we retreat and make a conscious effort to act the opposite way. Much of the time we aren't sure what the right way is."

We certainly weren't as compliant as our children would have wished. I, for one, was particularly recalcitrant.

My natural inclination is to hang on, not let go. Even the chores of motherhood that give me palpable pleasure, that seem to reaffirm the obligations of the office, are the ones that defy separation. Like name tapes. I love sewing on name tapes. The more socks the better. It appeals to my sense of order, to my love of the printed word, and most of all to my long apron strings. This child can never stray. Turn him or his sweater into the Lost and Found, and somehow he and it will find their way home. A latter-day Madame Defarge, I stitch my message in every sock and shirt: You are a Scobey, and don't you forget it. Mercerized cotton thread is my umbilical cord.

Sometimes the umbilical cord reaches farther than even I would dare hope. Here again is the older son, first-born and always eager for parental approval. When he got his driver's license at seventeen, liberating him not only from walking to school and public transportation but also from adolescence, we asked him to knock on our door when he came home at night. We didn't put curfews on his wheels. We didn't ask where he was going (he usually told us). There were no strings attached to his carburetor—only that he let us know when he returned. That way we could go to sleep at a decent hour and avoid the late-night pacing of our friends who had to ascertain their children's homecoming in more furtive ways.

"Sure," he said. And he faithfully knocked on our bedroom door, softly said, "I'm home," and we fell back to a deeper sleep. That courtesy went on through high school. And through college. And now, a graduate student in his twenties, he still stops by to knock on our door. No matter that he has arrived by train or that he's bringing a girlfriend home. I fully expect that when he brings his grandchildren to visit us, he will still stop by our room and dutifully whisper, "I'm home."

My husband, Rafe, has done his own share of resisting separation, and I well remember the day when both kids went off on a school ski trip during Christmas vacation. He turned to me and said, "Maybe we ought to buy a little ski place so the kids will want to spend their vacations with us." The idea was preposterous; we are not skiers, not second-home owners, and our idea of a terrific vacation is to play tennis or visit a foreign country, or, preferably, do both simultaneously.

"Listen," I said, "there's no need to bribe them with something we wouldn't enjoy. Just invite them to Greece or San Francisco or even a fall foliage weekend in New England. They'll be glad to spend time with us."

And indeed they were. Traveling *en famille* became standard procedure, so when we wanted to join a Peace March in Washington, we naturally took the children. Unlike many of our neighbors who traveled to Washington by a bus that left at 5:30 A.M., singing peace songs en route, we went by Metroliner at a respectable morning hour. At the time a round-trip ticket cost $25, and I remember thinking it would probably do more good just to send in the $100 and stay home.

How wrong I was.

We brought a picnic lunch and on that steamy ninety-degree

day we walked from Union Station, up Constitution Avenue to the Ellipse in back of the White House. We found a patch of unoccupied grass, edged close to a sheltering tree, and here we spread out the peanut butter and roast beef sandwiches and listened to Jane Fonda ("Greetings, fellow bums"). So we were counted among the 100,000 who turned out that Saturday in May to say something to their government about the Cambodian invasion and the Kent State killings. And we went home, having spent twice as much time in transit than we had on the ground. It wasn't a big deal. It was just something Rafe and I wanted to do—be counted. And we happened to take our children with us.

But it turned out that quite by chance we had said something more important to our children than we had to our government. As Rick said many years later, "By bringing us to the Moratorium, you showed us how much you respect us, how families must learn and share experiences together, how a family must unite to express itself."

When people took sides in the war, and so many of our friends found themselves in a more limited war with their children, there was no insurmountable breach at our house. We stood with our children. Was this why we escaped the sixties without being confronted with scruffy pony-tailed sons, emotional layabeds, or the greater tragedies of drug abuse? It's a simplistic answer, and so much of it surely rests on plain dumb luck. What if our children had been a year or two older and dumped into the middle of the rebellious protest that swirled around so many warm and caring families at the time? David was still in high school when the decade ended. Would he, faced with army service, have shot himself in the foot like one young man in town? Would he have gone to Canada, like several others we knew? Would he have enlisted in the Army, as still others did?

As it happens, when the time came to register for the draft and the large drum filled with birth dates tumbled and rotated, the long bony hand of the Selective Service System reached in and the third number to be picked was March 29. All boys born on March 29, 1954, found themselves with a Number 3. Good-bye, David Scobey.

"Not on your life," Rafe said to me. "Before that happens, we will all move to Canada."

"All? Us?" I asked. Ever since that child was seven, the possibilities of the Vietnam war had been tucked into a corner of my mind. Maternal worry is an anxiety I have perfected, and as the years went by and the war dragged on, it no longer seemed so outrageously neurotic to worry about a young boy eventually being sucked into the quagmire of Vietnam. And yet, all through the dread of what might be, of all the unacceptable choices that I foresaw, it never occurred to me that one solution was to move our whole family elsewhere. An astounding idea, to give up America. It wasn't as if we'd been here so long either—two generations on one side, three on the other. And it wasn't as if those European forebears hadn't fled their own atrocities. But to contemplate giving up American citizenship in the middle of the twentieth century?

It was much simpler to Rafe. "No question," he said firmly. "I'm not giving either of my boys to this war. And I won't have them going to Canada without us, like fugitives."

As it turned out—more dumb luck—the year David was required to register was the year the government gave up induction. He has his Selective Service card with its No. 003, and we never mentioned Rafe's alternate plan to him until a few months ago when somehow the subject came up.

"You'd have given up your law practice and moved to Canada?" He was incredulous.

"It would have been fun. We could have opened a bookstore," answered Rafe. "I always wanted a bookstore."

No answer from David. Just his hand moving across a corner of the dinner table to his father's, and a dampness in the eyes.

By now you may have noticed that we aren't a family that specializes in separations. What I began to notice in recent Septembers is that not many other families say good-bye well either. What most of us find out is that the shock of one's children leaving high school is as nothing compared to the trauma, several months later, of their actually moving out of the old homestead. That farewell sends a middle-aged message that can have startling ramifications.

Take Todd, whose oldest child, a daughter, has just left for college. He is inconsolable. The four remaining sons at home will not compensate. "Aging," he calls it, looking at it for the first time. But he grins sheepishly at the Freudian connection. Or Tom, a seemingly stable editor I know who also saw his daughter off to college. Despite the son still left at home, he lapsed into a despair of longing and loneliness. "Let's have another baby," he suggested to his working wife.

"Are you crazy?" she answered.

No sooner had I reported this astonishment to Rafe than he said, "I don't see anything funny about that. I'd love to have another baby." And, indeed, not long after, a forty-five-year-old man we know celebrated one child's graduation from high school with the birth of another.

To Dr. Saul E. Kapel, child-adolescent psychiatrist and associate professor, Cornell University Medical College, there is a clinical difference between a nostalgic yearning for another baby and really needing or having one. "The first is just a fantasy that relates to a man's longing and missing of his child," he says. "That's not serious. But if he means it literally, I suspect the fabric of the marriage is not very substantive and that the child kept the adults together. If a man needs a child to replace something that's missing, I would be suspect."

This replacement syndrome is a common form of compensation, says Elliott J. Rosen, a family therapist. In Rosen's view, the family is a carefully balanced system in which all members are interrelated, like gears in a watch. Remove one of the gears—as when a child leaves for college — and the remaining members find ways to make the family tick again. They try to redress the balance, reestablish an equilibrium, or, in Rosen's words, "seek a new homeostasis."

"Families have a life cycle," explains Rosen. "At each stage of the cycle, each person reorganizes: at the birth of the first child, the second child, children's independence, and so forth. For example, when the last child dresses himself and no longer needs the mother's constant attention, it's a common reaction to say, 'I want another baby.'"

However, when the last child ties his Adidas and jogs off to college, it isn't the mothers who want another baby. It's their mid-life fathers who, at that moment, feel particularly vulnerable. In his study of mid-life men, Levinson makes a fascinating observation: "Knowing that his own death is not far off, he is eager to affirm life for himself and for the generations to come. He wants . . . to bring something into being, to give birth, to generate life." The creation of a poem, a picture, an object can satisfy the generative impulse of mid-life men, Levinson believes, but clearly there are others whose instinct is literally to generate life.

Women seem to have rather different reactions to the same separation. "Mothers may feel the separation more acutely because they have more quantitative and perhaps qualitative time with children," says Kapel. "At least traditionally, and in the past, that's been true." Certainly the college departure is a signal of mortality, but for some women it has an added component of physical pain. Marie called me the day before her son left for school 3,000 miles away. "You didn't tell me how much it hurts," she wailed. "It's just like having a baby—nobody tells you that you ache for days." Marilyn reported a profound depression after her daughter left. "I couldn't understand it. I was doing interesting work of my own and looking forward to having more time for it. But for days I was tired down to my bones. I could barely get a cold supper on the table."

These are all parents who at least were aware of the coming separation. Pity our poor neighbors who suffered a triple whammy. Shortly before their twin sons left for college, the remaining child, a junior in high school, announced that he wouldn't be home that year either. While they had been looking at colleges with the twins, he had quietly been looking at boarding schools for himself. They were so busy making sure the college applications were submitted on time and enjoying the senior year activities of the older boys that they completely ignored the third child, figuring he'd be around for another two years. His startling announcement—"I'm certainly not going to be left home alone"—catapulted them into a mid-life trauma two years before they anticipated it.

How parents react when kids leave home reflects the quality of their relationship, says Kapel. "There are parents who are extremely attached to children and consciously or unconsciously need to hang on, even though the children are ready for that separation; they may indeed suffer. On the other hand, there are kids who have difficulty separating even though the parents are ready for them to go."

Our own first college separation turned out to be gentle; our older son was only going an hour away. But even though we could easily drive up, take him out for dinner, and be back well in time for the ten o'clock news, his very accessibility restrained us, and we probably saw less of him than other parents saw of their more distant offspring.

Besides, I promptly transferred all my maternal energies and attention to the remaining son, giving him the glorious chance to be an only child for three years. And when it was his turn to leave, I planned copiously for the impending crisis. I wasn't going to be caught like the Marilyns and Todds and Maries and Toms of this world. With well-honed neurotic anticipation, I started planning fully two years before the event. In addition to savoring each day as it passed irretrievably by—the next to last September 2, the next to last September 3, the last September 2, the very last September 3 —I would sign on to fill my own days with diverting activities from the moment we returned from delivering child, stereo, and cutoffs to the college of his choice. My own stab at homeostasis was not to have a baby or get a dog (a favorite replacement strategy), but to plunge into a frenzy of activity that would numb the pain of parting.

That isn't exactly the way it works.

The first thing you may have misgauged is the actual moment of parting. You take your youngest child to college, dump the guitar, the Adidas, and the blue jeans in the middle of the new room, and turn toward him for the Real Good-Bye. This is the moment you have anticipated. You want to mark the notable occasion in a worthy manner. Oh, nothing windy like Polonius's speech, just perhaps a loving and understanding squeeze of an arm. However, you are likely to find your child nervously eying not you but his new roommate and clearly wishing for your immediate departure. You suddenly realize that the real good-bye came earlier, perhaps at breakfast when you made his favorite pancakes, or when he paused at the front door for a long look back. After all your careful planning for this meaningful parting, you may have missed it altogether.

The next thing you may have misgauged is its duration.

4

WHOSE HOUSE
IS IT ANYWAY?

You have just installed your youngest child in his first really independent setting, and survived an awkward and unsatisfactory parting. By the time you get home and open your front door, miraculously you begin to see the flip side. You can reclaim the turf that for some years has been littered with the detritus of adolescence, and those other parts of your life that have been similarly encumbered. No longer will you have to ask permission to use the car on Saturday nights. You can pull out your best tie (sweater, blouse) without finding fresh tomato sauce on it (unless you're the one who's been to the pizza parlor), locate your tennis racquet exactly where you last put it, and that new can of balls, besides. Your friends can get through to you on the phone, and you won't have to make twice-daily trips to the supermarket. A lovely unaccustomed quiet is settling over everything. So long, Grateful Dead. Good-bye, Blondie. That famous empty nest may turn out to be just a pile of dried twigs after all.

Next you discover a beguiling spontaneity to your plans. You no longer need to be home at any particular time. In fact you no longer even need to call home. There's no one there to check on or check in with. (The main kink in your new free-floating timetable may be the damn dog you got to keep you company.) A six o'clock movie, which used to feel like playing hookie, now looks like excellent entertainment. Not to mention making love before dinner. Maybe not having dinner at all.

But before you can get your cozy new plan in high gear, your kid comes home for his first vacation. Your two-character romance is turning into a *Hellzapoppin* scenario.

Item: The kid is back and hogging the family car.

Item: Ditto the phone. Dad can't call home from his office, and he can't call out when he's home.

Item: The kid sleeps till noon and goes to the movies at midnight. What does he think this is, college?

Item: The kid does his/her laundry. Does he/ she also have to keep his/her room clean? Neat? Even if the door is kept closed at all times? Beyond telling us whether or not to expect them for meals, how much communication should we expect about their plans?

Item: You and your child never seem to be ready for the same meal at the same time. Your breakfast doesn't exist for your child. Your lunch may or may not be his/her breakfast. And the evening meal never seems in sync. As one friend of mine said, "I can get through the short vacations, even if it's an armed truce after the second day. But if he ever comes home to live, we'll have to put in another kitchen."

You'll notice there is a *déjà vu* about the issues. It's the circumstances that are different. The problem, of course, is that now there are more than two adults in the house. This raises fundamental questions. Whose rules? In fact, whose house is it anyway?

When the kids were young, there wasn't any question about who was in command. As they got older, they questioned our authority more and more. What started out as a benevolent dictatorship began to take on more of an egalitarian cast, at least in our house, as negotiations between the generations forced more equitable solutions. But still, until they left the old homestead to set up their own digs, our children generally accepted the fact that they were playing on our turf, with our ball. The significant differences came once they lived elsewhere, by their own rules.

All of this may aggravate us, but none of it should surprise us. Our post-high school children are in what Levinson calls the Early Adult Transition—a period when they start to separate from us and establish their own modus vivendi. The process, Levinson reminds us, "involves moving out of the familial home, becoming financially less dependent, entering new roles and living arrangements in which one is more autonomous and responsible . . . increasing differentiation between self and parents, greater psychological distance from the family, and reduced emotional dependency on parental support and authority." A big order. College, of course, is a splendid opportunity for all this testing and growing to begin, so conflict over whose rules and whose authority should be no surprise when our children return to the familial home from which they are trying to distance themselves. The conflicts are even sharper when children are finished with school and/or are working, and are obliged to live at home because they can't afford their own place.

In this tug-of-war over home rule, Gould offers a helpful perception: We retain our hold over our children not out of love or need to control but out of fear for our own safety. We aren't absolutely sure that when they leave our domain there will be a life for us. Is there life after children? It's a real question for those of us who have lived our entire life in a nuclear family. Says Gould, "Our children can't appreciate that this is our last family; they will go on to form a new family. We can't appreciate that after our children grow up and out, there's another life for us to lead."

As for our children, they, too, have apprehensions about life outside the nuclear family, both fearing and seizing their own independence. A return home, even for a short visit, tests their fragile autonomy. They suspect (with reason) that we will exercise our parental prerogatives with renewed vigor. No wonder every action is up for discussion, no item too inconsequential for debate.

You might regard the use of (a) the telephone, (b) the car, (c) the hours, and (d) the household responsibilities of these newly "grown-up" members of the family as open to differing opinions, even passionately differing opinions. But they are as nothing compared to the one issue that can cause the heat to rise without assistance from OPEC: the matter of bedfellows. What are the sleeping arrangements when a child brings home a Significant Friend?

Initial reactions commonly run the gamut of What? to *What?!* The response has little to do with the sex of the parent or with the sex or age of the principal. My friend Ginny reports that her eighteen-year-old son socked it to her before the first semester of his freshman year was over. The initial salvo seemed innocent enough.

"I'm coming home with my woman this weekend."

So Ginny readies the guest room for his woman (who, she reports, weighs eighty-six pounds). Then ensues this exchange:

Son: Why the two rooms?

Mother: I know from everything I've read that it's okay for me to say I'm putting you in two rooms because I don't feel comfortable otherwise.

That's the verbal part of the exchange. The nonverbal part occurred after her son and his woman went out for a walk. When Ginny passed the open door to his room, she saw in plain view on his desk an empty condom box. Furious, she threw it out . . . then carefully replaced the box in case the display was deliberate.

Ginny was much more forthright than a man I met who said he absolutely couldn't cope with the idea of his twenty-five-year-old daughter sharing her familial bed with a man. "It just isn't right," he said. My friend Laurie has her own view of why parents can't tolerate youthful cohabitation under the family roof. "It's not a moral question at all," she says firmly. "It's just too exciting for the parents. The fantasy of their child making love in the next room is too much for them to handle."

Absolutely right, says Gould. "Through our children, sex passes through our living room almost daily, waking us up and reminding us, through competition, envy, and jealousy, that it's still quite alive inside us." Levinson is more compassionate about our raging mid-life passions. "Parents too have growing pains; and they too need to be understood," he writes. "When a man's own aging weighs heavily upon him, his offspring's exuberant vitality is more likely to arouse his envy and resentment than his delight and forbearance."

If our growing pains are more pain than growth, we are likely to exacerbate family relationships. Take one neighbor of ours. She refuses to let her twenty-seven-year-old daughter or her twenty-four-year-old son share their rooms with the opposite sex. No matter that each child has been living with a Significant Friend for over two years. In her house they are not to sleep together. She figures they can abstain for one weekend. What happens is that neither child will spend the weekend with her. They come for the day, return to their own places at night. This was a tolerable arrangement when both children lived within an hour of her; it became thorny when each moved to another section of the country. Visits were few and far between, and Significant Friends were not included.

I'll say this for her domestic policy: There was no double standard. Hers was an equal opportunity household, with a lot more equality than opportunity.

If, on the other hand, our growing pains truly signify growth, we can give our children room (in every sense) to take responsibility for their own decisions. What's more, we are likely to find our own attitudes coming under reappraisal as our children compel us to confront those issues most of us haven't thought about since our own struggles for autonomy—those same thorny issues of sexual behavior and permissiveness that gave our own parents apoplexy a generation earlier.

Of the differing ways my generation comes to its sexual liberation, one of the best, it seems to me, is by learning from our children. My friend Rebecca has three sons, neatly spaced two years apart; her sentimental education has a nice developmental progression to it as each of her boys, in turn, established a serious relationship.

"When our oldest son brought his first girl home, we said to him, 'Lisa's room is upstairs, and you are not to go up without your clothes on.' " She roars as she remembers it. "God, it sounds absolutely Victorian."

The middle son did all his wooing in another state, and by the time the youngest son brought his girlfriend home, things had changed.

"It wasn't only that the times were different," recalls Rebecca, "and we had to grow with them just as much as our children did. But here was Andy living with Polly at school. It was ridiculous to say he couldn't sleep with her here. What's more," she added in her firmest ERA voice, "I'd feel exactly the same about a daughter."

My friend Dan is an even quicker study than Rebecca. His son was living with a new girl in the city, and his daughter was sharing a house with her good friend in Oregon in a relationship so permanent that even before their union was sanctified by law as well as by God they were filing joint tax returns as POSSLQ (an acronym devised by the Bureau of the Census to stand for Persons of the Opposite Sex Sharing Living Quarters). When Dan and his wife, Laurie, were offered the use of a friend's beach house, they generously invited their children, all POSSLQs included.

"Naturally," says Dan. "After all, they were all living together. Anything else would have been dumb. About a week before we were to leave, Hal said his girlfriend might not be able to come. 'Nonsense,' I said. 'Of course she'll come. We have the plane ticket and everything.'"

She went. And when the family arrived at the beach house, Dan announced the room arrangements. "Laurie and I in this room. Francie and Mike in that room. Hal and Julia in the other room. By the next day it was clear why Julia hadn't wanted to come—Hal and she were about to break up. Here I was, cool and sophisticated, assigning double rooms to my unmarried children—and they didn't even want to sleep together!"

Rafe and I got our chance to participate firsthand in the roommate dilemma, courtesy of David and the teaching assistant. Here's the background: Bright young college junior catches teacher's eye; she invites him to lunch. Pretty soon TA is teaching her student more than revivalism and the politics of slavery. And to tell you the truth, I thought it was terrific. Every young man should have a female mentor to initiate him into manhood with style, finesse, and flair. Besides, how else was the young poet to compose his Odes to Older Woman? And if I thought it was terrific, imagine how his father felt!

When David and the TA arrived one Friday for their first weekend *chez nous,* I left the room assignments to him. He installed his friend in the guest room. Whew! I thought. We're off the hook this time. In the middle of the night Rafe and I were awakened by the traffic in the hall. By Saturday night they had consolidated their camps and Rafe and I slept undisturbed. When we got up on Sunday morning, Rafe shrugged. "It's better than being awakened twice a night."

During the weekend I caught David alone and reminded him of a previous conversation. "Remember when you told me that sleeping together in the family home was for the parents and not for the children?"

"I said that?" he asked incredulously.

"You certainly did."

"I must have been talking about casual relationships. Not when two people really care for each other. Did our weekend upset you,

Mom? I put her in the guest room especially not to offend your sensibilities."

He did put her in the guest room. And he never said she wouldn't come out. I suddenly started to laugh, remembering my equal opportunity neighbor. Whatever made her think her children could abstain for a weekend? At their age, one night of love lost is lost forever.

As their friendship progressed through the fall and winter, I looked on it with continued amusement. But when David announced he wanted to move in with her that summer, the liaison didn't strike me as funny anymore.

"Listen," I said, trying to control myself. "You know I didn't say anything when you started this, but this is ridiculous."

"Don't get excited, Mother," he said. "We care for each other. We want to live together this summer. There are four other graduate students in the house, and we'll share the expenses. It's not that we want to get married or anything."

"Married? What kind of talk is that?"

"Calm down. I said of course we don't want to get married. I don't see what objections you have."

"You don't see what objections I have?" I sounded like a borscht circuit comic, repeating every statement as a question. "What does a woman like that want with a boy like you? She's twenty-eight. You're only twenty. What could she possibly want with you?"

"You make us sound obscene. It's not so strange. We hang around with graduate students. We share a lot of interests. We talk about philosophy and history and books and music. And when we go out together, I look like one more graduate student. Lots of men go out with women who are older."

"She's not just older. She's . . . she's . . . OLD."

"Oh, Mother." David shook his head sadly, and his eyes blurred slightly. He wanted so much to have me understand this major experience in his life. Not only understand it, but approve it. And I could barely discuss it rationally. What's more, I didn't even see that I was providing David with not one but two classic confrontations: I was forcing him to choose between two conflicting loyalties, between his mother and his woman, and in the process I was encroaching on his new and fragile sense of independence. No wonder our talks always ended disastrously. We were both hurt and angered by the breach. And if I persisted in my active disapproval or threw my hands up in sullen despair—either way lay danger. Warns Gould: "The child who follows our program of imperatives spends his/her adult life trying to escape the hell of never being able to live out his/her own life without guilt."

Wisely Rafe steered clear of these unsatisfactory discussions. He has a lawyer's patience and long-term view, and in the long run he didn't see this fledgling romance as causing any problems serious enough to undermine his basic support for his son. In the short run, I suspect that he enjoyed the macho adventure just as much as David.

"Listen, Joan," he said to me after one of their visits home. "She's certainly interesting to talk to—and she has great legs."

By the time June came around and the lovers moved into the Victorian house of graduate students, I knew I would accept the May/December summer. There are very few circumstances, if any, that can cause a fundamental rift between my children and me. This didn't seem to be one of them.

Considering the emotion I had invested in the love story, the denouement was embarrassingly undramatic. At the end of the summer, the teaching assistant went to a Midwest university as assistant professor; the junior became a senior and returned to his college dormitory. She led the life of a university professor, he of a university student, and the romance petered out via long distance, despite two or three cross-country weekends that made his mother nervous.

I recently asked David how he felt about the interlude. Now a graduate student (and a TA himself in the same department), he remembers it with pleasure. "It was a powerful experience. I was initiated into adulthood in a way that shortcut the bumbling. Besides," he added wickedly, "it was the closest thing to you, Ma."

Overlooking the Freudian dig, David's answer did give me a clue to the question I posed awhile back: Whose house is it anyway? It suddenly seemed clear. Most houses at least try to bend to the needs of all who live there. The difficulty is that the younger residents are now more articulate about their claims and the older ones fiercer about guarding their authority.

At this delicate juncture, each generation has painful responsibilities to the other. Our children must forge their own autonomy and separate from us without severing the relationship altogether. For our part, we have to relinquish parental control to accommodate that effort. As Levinson reminds us, we have to start "taking them seriously as adults, inviting their participation and fostering their growth toward greater independence and authority."

If we mid-life landlords hope to enjoy our progeny at home, we'd better call up our mutual trust and respect as we work out those issues that confront us. We'd better understand that the benevolent dictatorship of our early parenting is over, that all parties to the discussions now have equal standing. What's more, we'll have to come to terms with whether our newly adult children are required to carry a visa stamped with our values before they can take up residence in the homeland.

5

PPCV

We might be able to make a case for setting the ground rules in our own homes, but we're on shaky ground indeed when we try to export our lifestyle with our grown children. It isn't easy to keep hands off when they move onto paths of which we don't altogether approve. We're always facing the question of when—and if—we should intervene.

Some situations are clearer than others. For instance, acid heads seem to be a vanishing species, thank God, but young alcoholics—very young alcoholics—may be taking their place. That is alarming, and cause for intervention. On the other hand, what is one to do when a twenty-eight-year-old daughter calls home to say that (a) she is setting up a permanent household with a woman friend, and (b) she intends to bear a child and raise it in the single-sex home? This announcement, unexpectedly made to a couple I know, was so seismic that they instinctively knew they had to examine their own feelings before any discussion was possible. After their initial anguish, after reassuring themselves that their daughter had made her plans thoughtfully, they quietly accepted the reality. "There was nothing else to do," said the mother. "She's an adult, her lifestyle is completely alien to us, but we love her. I should say, *and* we love her. Besides," she added, "she has just given us our first grandchild."

Most of the time we're tempted to inject ourselves into decisions primarily because they collide with the aspirations we hold for our children: the son who eschews his father's business even though his help is badly needed; the daughter who chooses to forego college and marry her high school sweetheart. These may be disappointments, but not necessarily cause for intervention.

Hands off or not? There is usually a delicate balance, and more often than not we tip the scale in our favor. After all, we're the ones with the experience, the knowledge, the savvy, aren't we? But before we jump in with advice, if not consent, it's well to review our parental position at the time our children are just beginning to establish separate lives. First of all, as Gould reminds us, "It is hard for us to keep in mind that our young ones still overvalue our statements and opinions . . . and that we still want to hold on to our power over them."

Moreover, loss of power is yet another reminder of our advancing age. By the time our children are starting their independent lives, we are undeniably somewhere in that mid-life morass. We are beginning to understand in the most poignant ways that what our children do reflects on us. The choices they make, the lives they lead all validate our own choices and lives. As Levinson says of our offspring, "Their lives, their personal satisfactions, accomplishments and contributions are an essential part of [our] legacy." Small wonder, then, that we invest so much of our energy in seeing that they do right by us. "The joys and despondencies parents feel in middle age often seem excessive," Levinson observes. "The parents' preoccupations with 'how the children are doing' make more sense when seen in the context of the legacy: they reflect basic parental feelings about the value of one's contribution to posterity and one's claim on immortality."

I am reminded of my own legacy every night at ten o'clock when a local television station asks, "Do you know where your children are?" In central Africa, where our younger son is (and where, he hints, he is likely to spend a number of years), I don't even know when ten o'clock is.

This African genesis began when Rick was a senior in college and announced he was applying for a post in the Peace Corps.

The Peace Corps?

"That was for the 1960s," I said. "Who's doing that anymore?"

"I am," he answered. "I had an interview with the Peace Corps recruiter at college, and it reminded me what a wonderful experience it would be. It's exactly what I want to do. I want to be on my own, to test myself."

"Have you considered VISTA?" I suggested, referring to the

government's domestic version of the Peace Corps. "You could learn wonderful things about yourself and about this country, about alien cultures on an Indian reservation, about ecology and survival in the Northwest, about . . ."

"You don't understand, Mom. I don't want to be near a phone."

"I promise I won't call."

"No, it isn't you. It's me. I don't want to be able to call you or a friend if something goes wrong. I want the challenge of really testing myself."

"You're willing to put two years into it?"

"Yes."

What, I wondered, was this preppy going to do in the Peace Corps? His idea of high adventure was to swing up Fifth Avenue, hand in hand with a twinkly lass, and end up at the Palm Court of the Plaza Hotel for scones and tea.

"You're prepared to be nine thousand miles from Haägen-Dazs ice cream and David's Cookies?"

"Boy, you sound just like my friends. They can't believe I'm doing it either. But what I ask them is, don't they realize that the preppy from Brown has a whole other side?"

Of course, I knew that the Brown preppy had many other sides; I just wasn't prepared for the breadth and decisiveness of his statement of independence. No mere wire hanger around the neck for him. He may be the textbook example of what psychologists call "separating": moving physically, psychologically, economically, emotionally—in every way—away from one's parents. He was following to perfection the developmental task that Levinson describes for young men between seventeen and twenty-two: "shifting the center of gravity of his life; no longer a child in his family of origin, he must become a novice adult with a home base of his own."

Coming to terms with a home base in Africa is not easy. It's not that I disapproved exactly, but I certainly wish it were different. This is my youngest, the delightful playmate with whom I laugh and explore and cook and gossip, who will be out of voice contact for two years. Intervention crossed my mind, but I suspected I would have very little to say about his decision.

What I did discover is that many parents were interested in our reaction—not in what the child was doing but in how we handled it. The following conversation occurred frequently. The opening question is typical—and I finally understood it referred more to their children than to our son—but the observations are by a woman psychiatrist.

"What did you do when your child said he wanted to go?"

"Nothing. I figured I didn't have anything to say. He's twenty-two. He thought it out carefully. I hate his going but I trust his judgment."

"But what did you *say?*" she persisted.

"Nothing," I repeated.

"You're not hearing me."

"I hear you."

"No, you may be listening, but you're not hearing me. I know plenty of people who tell their grown children what to do."

I probably would have, too, I realized—if I thought I could have gotten away with it. But the truth is, I envy him. It sounded like a great adventure. I finally realized what the trouble was—it was me I felt terrible for.

Besides, his father supported the choice enthusiastically. "Every young man should have a vision of the world, a sense of wonder, and a chance for adventure," he said firmly. There went my only ally.

It was clear that I'd better learn, and fast, to cope with this quintessential separation. The lengthy application process helped. And as Rick sorted through his choices, I tried to raise my middle-aged sensibilities, which had been weaned on One World, to Third World consciousness.

Sierra Leone—Community Health Worker. He passed this up because of the steamy tropical monsoon climate and not, he swears, because of the accommodations. ("The house will not have electricity or running water but will have a cement floor, an outside latrine, and a zinc pan roof.")

Chile—Rural Nutrition or Health Promoter. Rafe eliminated both of these on grounds of politics, and I was relieved that the infuriatingly wise hands-off father wasn't above limiting Rick's choices when they offended his sense of democracy and/or safety.

This left two placements in Malawi. No, Malawi is not a small island in the Pacific belonging to Hawaii, as we first thought. It is a small slice of country at the southern end of East Africa, poking a long inquiring finger into Mozambique. One placement was Environmental Sanitation Worker. His father, like any Army veteran, knew just what that meant. By the time Rick read "Experience and interest in construction work highly desirable," he had a clearer idea, too.

"Oh," he said. "Shoveling shit."

Building latrines was not exactly the adventure he had in mind, and that's how, by default, he became an Adult Literacy Officer.

While his college classmates were scheduling interviews with recruiting corporations and studying for the LSAT, GRE, GMAT, and other acronyms that help graduate schools populate themselves, Rick was learning the alphabet soup and jargon for his new career. To help Rafe and me understand his new life, he instructed us in one of his two foreign languages (the other is Chichewa, the native dialect).

"PCTs [Peace Corps trainees] go to a PRIST [preinvitational staging] where they learn about HCNs [host country nationals]. If a PCT gets approved by PCW [Peace Corps Washington], he goes overseas and after more training finally becomes a PCV [Peace Corps volunteer]. In addition to our PST [preservice training], we also receive IST [in-service training] on a variety of issues such as BHN [basic human needs], TEFL [teaching English as a foreign language], and PQLI [physical quality of life index]. Once a year we fill out a VAS [volunteer activity survey] in which we discuss how well we are realizing PC 'Basicness Criteria.'"

"GG! [Good Grief!!]"

By the time Rick came home from his CAST (center for assessment and training) in the hills of Kentucky, we knew we'd have to speed up our own training as PPCV [parents of Peace Corps volunteer].

How do you say good-bye to a beloved child for two years? This is not an entirely new experience for us, but I never seem to get it right. As George Eliot said, "In every parting there is an image of death." We've already had practice with a long-term filial farewell: to the older son, off to study in England for three years. We drove him down to the ship (he was going in style on the *Queen Elizabeth*

39

2) and the glamour of the occasion somewhat diverted us from the poignant parting. But when he went up the gangplank and the commanding whistle of the tugboats cut the early evening air, the enormity of the separation hit me.

"I'll never see him again," I sobbed to Rafe.

"Don't be ridiculous," he said. And, of course, it wasn't long before I discovered that there was adequate postal service, indeed even telephone communication, with that distant isle.

Now, however, I am facing two years in the African bush. Telephones? Don't count on it. I'm not even sure of the postal service. I have a very primitive notion of the whole undertaking, fostered in large part by the Peace Corps' own description of its outposts. ("In some mountain villages you may not see a Western peer for a year.")

I am readying for an October departure. The first thing I notice every morning on wakening is a physical jolt. A knot in the stomach. Something's wrong, but what is it? Oh, yes, Rick is leaving. A chronic physical ache. Nausea. It's the mid-life version of morning sickness, the physical pain of separating a mother from a child.

Countdown begins officially in September. Farewell weekend No. 1, David comes down from New Haven, Denise up from Washington. Farewell weekend No. 2, David comes down from New Haven, Denise up from Washington. Farewell weekend No. 3, David down . . .

And then his departure date is postponed until January 3. O frabjous day! Callooh! Callay!

I'm the only one, it turns out, who is delighted by the reprieve. Rick is eager to go. David and Denise are tired of traveling Amtrak. Rafe feels he has already said good-bye more than enough times.

I, however, am looking forward to farewell weekends Nos. 4 through 16. Not to mention our last Thanksgiving and our last Christmas together. I'm really getting into the swing of these maudlin gatherings. I'm not exactly crying all the time. It's just that my eyes are forever leaking.

"It's not that I don't want you to go," I keep assuring Rick. "It's just that I feel terrible for me."

Rick, meanwhile, is spending his last weeks saying farewell to persons and things of consequence to him, and imprinting the taste of pasta, bagels, and chocolate mousse indelibly on his palate. And when the list of suggested equipment arrives ("See, it's just like camp, Ma." "Boot camp, you mean."), he shops for the essentials: a backpack, tape recorder plus tapes of the best-loved music, and a shortwave radio, the umbilical cord to his civilization.

"Don't you need to take any toiletries?" I ask.

"No. Peace Corps supplies all the essentials—aspirin, condoms, and dental floss."

His main assignment, on advice of Peace Corps, is the removal of his four wisdom teeth. The oral surgeon instructs me in the postoperative care and I throw myself into it enthusiastically. The swollen jaws, the bloody gauze that needs frequent changing, the puking after each sip of ginger ale—even the ginger ale itself, lovingly administered through the bent straw—remind me I haven't been a mother-nurse in years. A warm delicious sense of neededness warms me. The poor boy is near-comatose, bloody—and some not so small corner of my mind is enjoying it with deep-felt satisfaction.

In body and psyche, the child was now well prepared for the adventure. Not so the mother. It wasn't the malaria notice ("You are scheduled to serve in an area where malaria is prevalent") that unnerved me as much as the request for complete dental X rays and fingerprints.

It didn't make things any easier when I caught an ad for Mary McCarthy's book, *Cannibals and Missionaries,* on the food page of *The New York Times.*

Nor when my friend Jim told me about an agronomist he knows who was learning an African dialect in preparation for a trip to Mali. "By the second lesson, he could greet the natives," reported Jim. "In the fifth lesson he could name twelve fatal illnesses that plague the country. And by the twelfth lesson he was conjugating verbs, and had learned the passive voice—using the verb 'to eat.'"

When we finally arrive at the last family dinner, Rick, historically the family caterer, insists on making it. We find a gift at every seat, and with each there is a note, a summing up of relationships. At my place a basket of four African violets, each variety with a name. The violets for the continent that will harbor him for these coming years; one for each of the four rooms I most use. The note: *Talk to them when needed—they won't talk back.*

"Well, Julie," I say to the pink one in the kitchen as I'm washing the dishes, "it's going to be a long winter."

Then one day in the middle of Christmas week, Rick reminds me: "Tony and Bill will be here pretty soon."

"Tony and Bill?" These are unfamiliar names.

"Tony from New Mexico, Bill from Colorado. I met them in training at the CAST. They're going to Malawi with me. Remember I told you I had invited anyone in the group to stay over here when they get to New York for the flight?"

Naturally, I had repressed the whole conversation.

"The kids from California and the Southwest will be coming to town the day before we leave," he reminds me. "They can't do the flight in the same day. You don't mind, do you?"

I hesitated. I goddamn did mind.

"It will be really nice for you to meet the people I'll be with for two years," he says.

That's true. I require a complete and detailed picture of my family's life in faraway places. Not just the people they work and play with, but the mailbox to which my weekly letter will be delivered, and the chair and coffee mug that are likely to witness its reading. A detailed sense of place goes a long way to reassure me.

"It's okay as long as they understand that we're driving you to the airport *alone.*" I don't want anyone mucking up the last Last Farewell. I've been working up to it for months.

On January 2 the PC crew start arriving. All day long they arrive. Not just Tony and Bill. By dinner time there are twelve of them. We've gotten an all-American dinner together for an expandable crowd: chili, rice, beer. And what with the friends of the friends who have appeared, there isn't even room at the dinner table for us. What was literally to be our farewell dinner with Rick and a couple of Peace Corps colleagues turns into an inauguration of their adventure.

David and Denise, Rafe and I take our chili plates into the living room. We hear loud nervous laughter from the dining room as twelve strangers feel each other out, knowing they had better like one another.

"I thought we were going to have our last dinner together," I say, my voice high and thin. "But they're taking him away a day early . . ." Tears plop into my chili.

"I hate them all," says Denise.

I'd like to tell you that the airport farewell the next day was wrenching, heartbreaking. The fact was that it was hectic, confused, feverish. And as soon as we drove out of the airport precincts, the headache I had had for three months miraculously lifted.

"Thank God it's over," I said. "Now we can all get on with our lives."

I may have spoken too soon. It wasn't a year before we followed Rick to the bush. We weren't able to let our baby have his African adventure all by himself. We had to take a look at it. And what we learned was that letting go and trusting one's child really do have their own rewards. I don't mean just the sense of wonder at the primeval landscape of Rick's corner of Africa, which we would never have seen otherwise. I don't even mean the delight at seeing one's child rely on himself and build a life in an alien culture, at watching him make his Malawian colleagues laugh in their own Chichewa dialect. Nor the deep sense of satisfaction in knowing that he could make his way in the world without the sheltering presence of his parents.

What we really began to perceive in that remote region (there's nothing like that dawn-of-man landscape to bring on big thoughts) was that there was plenty to learn from a child. That, freed from the custodial relationship, we were now enjoying him as a fellow grown-up, with all the possibilities that promised. That, paradoxically, geographic distance was fostering closeness, that separation was just as maturing for the middle-aged parents as for the offspring. That our children's steps to autonomy could pave our own path to mid-life independence. That without our children to nurture, fuss over, guide, we could indeed rely on ourselves and take comfort in our own ability to survive. There seems to be life after children, after all.

6

COUPLING

Getting on with a newly child-free life provides some surprising paradoxes. The first one is likely to be sexual. Just as we're feeling older and bemoaning our years, we're also feeling younger, sprightlier, and sexier than we have in a long time. This renewed sexual vigor may catch us with our pants down, but it's no surprise to the psychologists who monitor our development. "When the children leave home altogether," observes Gould, "we experience a greater release from inhibition. . . . We're also spurred on by envy and jealousy of their youthfulness, their shapeliness, their sexuality and their opportunities in life."

For years we have been virtually asexual—or at least furtive—when our children are in the house. Our sex lives are typically confined to a darkened bedroom, the door securely shut. Suddenly we can leave the lights on, the doors open, the pajamas off. We may not move our sexual encounters to the kitchen floor or under the piano (as a sex therapist once suggested for erotic interest), or paint *I Love You* on our abdomens (as one newly liberated husband did, according to his startled wife), but we certainly feel a new lack of restraint in our sexual activity.

"If we can abandon our inhibiting parental roles, our sex life suddenly improves," continues Gould. "Our parental inhibitions come from a childhood consciousness belief that parents are essentially asexual." And who doesn't have an unshakable certainty in the virginity of one's parents—despite the tangible evidence of oneself? My mother and father? Never! In our own parental roles, we convey the same information to our children. We tend to act decorously with them.

"As they grow older," writes Gould, "we show them more, and

each of us remembers finding out bit by bit about our parents' secret personalities." Indeed. I believe I was more shocked to discover as a child in grade school that my mother the lawyer not only loved parties and singing but wasn't above dancing on the piano than I was as a married woman to find out that my parents—the very same mother and father who didn't do that sort of thing—had slept together before they were married. (Shrugged my father, "Your grandmother made the mistake of putting me in the guest room right next to your mother's.")

Our newfound heady abandon also has its down side in the incidence of impotence. Dr. Maj-Britt Rosenbaum, psychiatrist and director of the Human Sexuality Center, Jewish-Hillside Medical Center, Long Island, commonly counsels middle-aged men. "It can be a shock when a middle-aged man suddenly loses his potency," she says. "It threatens his marriage and his sense of self. Impotence is not just sexual; it threatens life potency."

Impotence has causes other than psychological. In the acute population that Rosenbaum sees, she estimates that organic problems account for one-quarter to one-half of the cases. Drugs and medications also cause impotence; however, the medications are often prescribed for conditions common to middle age-high blood pressure, anxiety, depression, ulcers—and similar circumstances might not trigger impotence in younger men, she believes.

"There is the need to be able to adapt to the changes and stresses of mid-life," says Rosenbaum. "Talking out the problem with one's wife can lead to real rejuvenation of the relationship. Sexuality can be renewed or experienced for the first time."

Our new concern with sexuality suggests that changes are taking place in the marriage. And indeed, when our children leave home, there is a lot more than sexual preoccupation going on. The whole nature of the institution is different. We are now essentially a childless unit, not just a shadow of our former family but an entirely different organism. We have completed our purpose as a family: to bring up children. Now we face more than endings; we face beginnings. A profound sense of loss, an underlying sense of challenge and, yes, nervousness. Nervousness because the familiar shifting and balancing act that has always kept the family momentum going no longer seems to be working. Small adjustments and accommodations that formerly filled the interstices no longer redress the imbalances. As Gould says, "When the children leave home, the whole marital arrangement has to be restructured."

And now more than ever. The Compleat Couple who, in our parents' day appeared to march in lockstep, discovering together the joys of a child-free life, now more often than not find themselves buffeted by their individual, competing needs. "Issues of intimacy and freedom, for example, which are supposed to concern young adults just starting out in marriage and careers, are never settled once and for all," observes Neugarten. "They haunt many couples continuously; compromises are found for a while, then renegotiated."

The components of these tug-of-war relationships are embarrassingly stereotypical, but no less real for their familiarity. As Neugarten points out, "Most of the themes of adulthood appear and reappear in new forms over long periods of time." At this particular mid-life juncture, more often than not they center on each partner's yearning for autonomy (in an ironic parallel to the simultaneous struggle their children are making). The mid-life husband and father, whose emotional and financial burdens are considerably lessened, may want to cut back on his working life, spend time developing interests that had to be put aside, do things that are simply more interesting or more fun than how he has been spending his days. The non-work-a-day world looks extraordinarily appealing.

For mid-life wife and mother, however, that's precisely the milieu she is looking to flee. If she hasn't been employed while her children were at home, she's likely to feel she has spent more than enough time developing her interests between 8:30 and 3:30. She's been waiting long enough to get back in what she is wont to call the "real world." If she's been juggling job and children, full-or part-time, she welcomes the simplification of a child-free state and the chance to focus full-beam on her career, whether it is paid employment, volunteer, or academic. With each partner exploring new interests, often headed in opposite directions, there is potential for trouble. A lot of rebalancing must be done to reestablish that homeostasis. And there are many roads to working out the pulls and tensions that beset so many mid-life marriages.

Sometimes the road ends in a fork, and each partner follows a different path out of the woods. Take Hank and Helen. Helen left home the minute the last child left for college. She had married young, and Hank was twelve years older. She had never lived anywhere by herself. She went from her mother's home to her husband's home. Now, feeling acutely abandoned by her children, she had a driving need to go out on her own, to test herself. It almost seemed as if she needed to establish the independent self she hadn't had time for as a young adult. So as soon as her youngest son packed his T-shirts and went to school, Helen packed her city suits and said good-bye to Hank. She found an apartment, got a job with a magazine, began making new friends, and occasionally went out on dates when her married friends had unmarried friends.

Helen's behavior seemed precipitous to her pals, but it falls into a familiar mid-life pattern according to psychologist Gould. "As we redefine ourself and our old relationship, we dream of being alone, and we ask, *What would I be like if I hadn't married her or him?* This leads to a series of experiments," he writes, "such as taking courses, meeting new friends, reestablishing old rusty relationships, and doing what we've always been hesitant to do because he or she would disapprove or think it silly."

After a year on her own, Helen had enough of being alone. She was often lonely. She didn't like going out at night by herself. Most of the men she met would tell her obsessively about the glories of stewardesses and "young flesh." Fun City wasn't nearly as much fun as she had anticipated. And her day-to-day friends—that famous support system—were back at the old hometown. She hadn't solved her problems, she had just exchanged them. Like the old saying, she preferred the devil she knew to the devil she didn't know. She began to understand that she could grow as an individual within the confines of a marriage. She returned to Hank.

Hank and Helen discovered that sometimes those separate paths through the thickets do converge in a clearing on the other side. That some marriages do improve after one or both partners get some distance and a little self-understanding. Even—maybe especially—if those wanderings are adulterous. That certainly seems the case with Claire, a college classmate. Just as the last of her children was about to leave for college, she began fluttering aimlessly in her near-empty nest, perched precariously in what she felt was a humdrum marriage. Typically, most of her friends in the same situation dove into frenzied activity. Some took jobs, others went back to school, and a few got into volunteer work via social agencies, museums, hospitals, whatever. None of that attracted Claire. Also typically, Claire was moving toward an extracurricular dalliance. As Gould points out, "Often our adventures are sexual, since they are usually the most forbidden."

"I knew it was going to be a bad time," Claire remembers of that emptying-nest summer. "In a way I was preparing for it. Without my consciously realizing it, I was sending messages to men. All of a sudden, men became much more attentive to me. They invited me to lunch and, well, even propositioned me." She shook her dark hair and laughed at the old-fashioned word.

"One weekend I went to a convention with Jack, and we met a really nice man—divorced—who had his own company in Chicago. A few weeks later he came east on business and called me. I had lunch with him and, well, we saw each other after that every time he came to town. It went on through the summer.

"And when Billy left for school in September, I simply left home one day and went to Chicago. Oh, I didn't sneak out on Jack —I told him I had to get away. I just couldn't cope with the empty house and the empty talk at dinner and the generally empty feeling I had. I just flew to this lovely man in Chicago who thought I was wonderful. One day we were at a museum and he ran into a friend of his. The guilt and the shame made me feel like a big scarlet neon *A* was blinking on and off on the front of my blouse. I asked him how he felt about . . . us . . . being seen together. He smiled and said, 'I thought, Eat your heart out, Sam.' "

How long did it last? I ask Claire, who long since flew back to the old coop.

"It was over very quickly—really only five or six days," she says. "Of course, when I left I didn't know when, or if, I'd be back. But as soon as I got to Chicago, there was a tremendous pull to go home. It wasn't the guilt. It was a real sense of loss. A need to be attached. And, partly, it was the gnawing feeling of what I was doing to Jack and the kids. But mostly it was the commitment I have to our family, and to the part of it that is ClaireJack. You know, I always felt that there was Claire and there was Jack and there was also a big part of our marriage that was ClaireJack. I didn't want to abandon ClaireJack."

So Claire came home, and what she once perceived to be humdrum began to feel comfortable and loyal. And safe. There was a lot of working out to do, she reports, especially with the children. But that brief rupture gave her the distance to view her marriage in a different way, and to begin to value its importance and strength, most especially, she says, in mid-life.

Sue Ellen and Walt found an equally radical solution to the tensions of their mid-life marriage: they reversed roles. Sue Ellen is a science writer. While her children were young, she free-lanced from home. Walt was an advertising copywriter who worked at a dizzying pace. When their children became relatively self-sufficient, Walt opted for early retirement, and Sue Ellen raced out of the house to a staff post on a newspaper. They didn't merely exchange places of business; they exchanged responsibilities. Sue Ellen rode off on the 7:42 each morning to her big city desk and weekly paycheck. Walt went marketing before playing in his dark room, and prepared dinner while Beethoven string quartets filled the eat-in kitchen. They were now, at last, living out their independent dreams.

The arrangement that Sue Ellen and Walt arrived at in mid-life was no more startling than their young-married personae. Sue Ellen is a genteel Southerner who loves poetry, flowers, and proper tea. She would wear white gloves and a floppy hat to a garden party if only one of her friends would give one. She doesn't care much about food and never learned to cook; there was no need to in Daddy's house and, as it turned out, no need to in Walt's house either. Walt is an urban ethnic who loves food and cooking. A peek into his refrigerator would reveal eleven kinds of mustards and several exotic Eastern roots and sauces. He reads spy novels and cheers the Cleveland Indians. It appeared to their friends that what Walt and Sue Ellen mainly had in common were three children and the need for a typewriter. They also turned out to have that rare gift: the ability to stabilize each other's flights, to teeter when the other tottered, to counter a centripetal force with a centrifugal action. An odd coupling that together formed a strong and stable unit.

Dramatic mid-life changes like swapping lifestyles, leaving

home, or trying a little adultery aren't the only catalysts for mid-life marriage appraisals. Our own marriage came under scrutiny for much more prosaic reasons. It began with a late-night telephone call.

"Hey, Ma," announced the deep voice. "Denise and I set our wedding day!" It's not exactly a surprise, mind you. A young man who for three years spends every available minute with the same young woman might be expected to have a permanent liaison in mind. Nevertheless, the news is startling—to David, I think, as well as to us. Suddenly strange phrases and concepts bubble up. *Mother-in-law. In-laws. Grandma!?*

Dinner-table conversations, which formerly rambled from the weakness of the New York Giants' offensive line to the First Amendment rights of students now focus on the rehearsal dinner and the relative merits of sit-down versus buffet for the wedding repast. Here is this bearded radical historian, the fellow I expected would recite a love poem of his own composition under an apple tree at his back-yard wedding, weighing navy jacket versus dark suit for the nuptials. The scholar himself smiles sheepishly and confides to his future mother-in-law, "I don't like this whole business of being engaged, but I love being a fiancé."

Nevertheless, with all the advance warning we had, and the happiness we feel at their marriage, the phone call announcing they had set a date was curiously unnerving. Nothing had changed in our relationship with David and Denise, and everything had changed. Loyalties were subtly shifting. No longer would Rafe and I be David's primary family, and it gave me pause as I was about to pass on a family confidence. Did Denise have the right now to our family's privileged information? Did we have the right to ask him not to share it?

But primarily that late-night phone call was a dramatic mid-life proclamation for the parents. What more decisive reminder can you have that you are no longer twenty-seven than that your twenty-seven-year-old son is getting married? It not only clearly defines the generations, but it also calls into review the state of one's own marriage. This evaluation, as it turned out, was being made at the same time by the young couple.

Here is David's report of their interview with the rabbi (who probably thought he was interviewing them). The rabbi was interested, not in the mechanics of the ceremony or whether Denise would or wouldn't promise to obey, but whether they intended to remain a family unit until death do them part. In the course of that discussion, the rabbi asked them to rate the marriages of their parents: poor, fair, good, or excellent.

"How did you rate us?" I ask.

"Good."

"Why only good?"

"It's impossible for a child to regard his parents' marriage as excellent," David answers. "We're there through thick and thin. We see it all. We bear the consequences of it. What the rabbi really wanted to know was what we saw to emulate and what to avoid."

"Oh? What was that?"

"Well, I know I want to avoid your temper and Dad's lack of easy responsiveness. I want Denise and me to be involved as parents every day, not just a daily Mother presence and a Father's remote philosophical hand."

"What did you want to emulate?"

"The fact that you regarded us as friends, were open enough to learn from us. The way you talked with us at the dinner table—that was very important—and taught us how to listen. You took us seriously. You enjoyed our friends."

"Does Denise feel the same way?" (What I really want to know is how she rated her parents.)

"Yes, very much so. She said her parents' marriage was good, too. Mostly for the same reasons. Plus the closeness of her parents' friends and their children. There was a network of multigenerational families caring about each other."

That night, before repeating David's story about the rabbi to Rafe, I ask him to evaluate our marriage, using the same grading system.

"Good," he says.

"Why only good?" I explode.

"No marriage is excellent." Looking at my crestfallen face, he tries to make amends. "It's extraordinarily good, amazingly good, fabulously good."

But still not excellent.

Well, what does make a good (if not excellent) marriage? I put the question to two friends. Barbara answers quickly, "Communication."

"Oh, no," says Nancy. "Some of the best marriages I know depend on not communicating too much."

"I'd like to think it's a passionate friendship," adds Barbara.

"Clearly," says Nancy, reversing Tolstoi, "happy families don't resemble one another at all."

Perhaps not in style, but they do have similar ingredients. The ability to change—or at least accept change in one's spouse—seems to be an essential component. "Ideally, in a really happy, really adult marriage," says Gould, "change in one partner is met gladly by the other partner, who is not afraid of the growth, but welcomes it—intellectually, at least—as an interesting improvement in the relationship."

Accommodations take place at many levels. There are what Barbara calls "big permissions for growth," and these surely require a sturdy sense of self because both grantor and grantee are likely to suffer during the realignment process. Accommodation also accords a fair degree of privacy and separateness, not crowding one's companion, respectfully allowing individual growth in what our children like to call "my space." Beyond this, most marriages, it seems to me, rest most of the time on small permissions, those daily adjustments that are needed to keep the machine going.

How each of us performs the large and small balancing acts that keep our marriages in equilibrium is uniquely personal, but those marriages seem to share a similar mix. The ones I admire, at least, rest in varying degrees on good will, respect, love (whatever that is), sex, and humor—lots of humor. And when you put all that together there must still be room for muddling through, for grinding down the flinty edges, for fine-polishing the courtesies and civilities, for adjudicating the important disputes, like who forgot to turn out the light or ran out of gas.

This being the eighties, the mid-life couples I know have disputes unknown to their parents (and that will be foreign to their children as well). These couples are caught between the women's movement, with its demands (expectations?) for self-fulfillment, employment, and equality, and the old marriage contract. My husband, for instance, didn't sign up to do the dishes. It's not that he won't; it's simply that he doesn't. The route to and from the dining room is via the living room, not the kitchen.

Long ago I realized I had to decide what I wanted to make an issue of. (My natural inclination is to make an issue of every issue.) Here's how the dishwashing issue went:

"Hey, how about helping with the dishes?"

"Sure, as soon as the news is over." By the time the news was over, there was a segue into the "Game of the Week," and Himself had long since forgotten any appointment in the kitchen.

"For God's sake! Can't you ever help with the dishes?"

"Sure. All you have to do is ask."

It didn't take me more than ten or twelve years to realize that not every thread in the family fabric carries the same weight. So I lowered my expectations.

"Hey," I call out nightly, as the evening news anchor greets his viewers, "you forgot to take your plate into the kitchen."

As everyone knows by now, young wives and mothers today have more to say about the shape of their marriages than we did. We took on our husband's persona so completely that our maiden names often did not survive as a middle initial, let alone as our identifying surname. Just how much more young wives have to say was something I learned when I drove David and Denise to the airport one day and, as chauffeur, overheard this conversation. (To appreciate the dynamics, you need a little background. David is an academic, working on a doctorate and hoping to spend a productive professorial life. Jobs are scarce in academe. Denise is an economist. Of the two, she is likely to be the major breadwinner. David's contribution will be more time at home, or at least more flexibility. It's a given that they will share the child rearing. What is under discussion are jobs for David if he can't find one teaching.)

"What about consulting—say for an urban planning agency?" David suggests.

"That might be interesting," says Denise. "We'd be able to find a city where we could both work."

"And there might be a lot of traveling," adds David enthusiastically.

"Hey, then I veto that," says Denise firmly. "You can't be away from home too much."

When Rafe and I made our marriage contract, there was no discussion of where we would live (near his job) or how much he would travel (whenever necessary). Our nuptial covenant was notable for the omissions, not the stipulations. It didn't specify the maker of the beds (me), the taker of the shirts (me), the raker of the leaves (him). It didn't designate who buys the food (she) or wine (she) or clothes, even his (she). When we made our contract, there were no clauses. We pledged to love and honor, and no more.

I'm not at all sure this was a bad arrangement. Without the constraints of premarriage compacts and articulated demands—or even a lot of anticipatory discussion—we had plenty of room to maneuver, to accommodate, to modify. I often get to rake the leaves (too often) and he occasionally gets to take out the shirts (too occasionally). And sometimes neither of us makes the beds.

We're even making progress on those more difficult accommodations—the emotional ones. Take that lack of "easy responsiveness" that David talked about. Because Rafe has never been demonstrative, I am always tempted to smother him in pinches and hugs and declarations of love. Publicly, of course.

"Oh, cut it out," he begs.

"So why don't you ever whisper sweet nothings, declare yourself romantically?"

"God, Joan."

"Why don't you tell me you can't live without me, write me mash notes . . ."

"Cut it out." Here comes the big romantic declaration: "You know that without you I'd still be walking up five flights to a one-room apartment."

When I gather my love letters together, there may be only one yellowing entry. It accompanied a dozen roses, and it was written sixteen years ago by a California florist: *All my love, Mr. Scobey.* Now, when I seem to be edging into a lovelorn complaint, Rafe will remind me of the couple I used to hold up to him as a model of devotion: the man who gazed soulfully at his wife playing love songs on the guitar—just before he ran off with his secretary.

54

This grass-is-greener syndrome seems to afflict even the best of mid-life marriages, as I noticed at a recent party. It happened to be Valentine's Day and, in a mid-life commentary on hearts-and-flowers, after dinner the husbands gravitated to one side of the living room, the wives to the other.

Says Mary to the women, "If you could marry again, what would you look for?"

Lynn, married to a lovely history professor to whom she is devoted, says, "I'd look for money."

Josie, who has a lot of money and a husband three inches shorter than she who makes her laugh a lot, says, "Tall. I'd look for tall."

Mary looks over at her husband, a six-foot-two stockbroker and says, "Rich and tall isn't enough. There's got to be more to life than that."

After we all laughed (a little nervously; was Mary serious?), I considered what passes for valentines among the more stable marriages we know. The mid-life valentines usually have nothing whatever to do with February 14, except that they come from the heart. Our friend Jules, for instance, is a television producer who moved from New York to California, where first wives of twenty-five years' standing are an endangered species. Always a man of the soil, he is wont to present Dorothy on memorable occasions with a flowering shrub for their patio.

Jim, perhaps tiring of hearing Judith say, "Oh, my aching back," recently brought home a whirlpool for the bathtub. The fact that she feared being electrocuted by the damn thing was no reflection on Jim's devotion. Now he has taken to booking a hotel room in town when they have theater tickets, exactly the kind of valentine a suburban wife appreciates. As Judith says, "Thank heaven Jim is sharing his mid-life crisis with me!"

My own favorite valentine is not the dozen roses that came so many years ago (they were prompted not so much by affection as by fright at having lost control of a car after carousing with clients in the Hollywood hills) but a cartoon Rafe clipped from *The New Yorker* magazine. It distills all the nuances of our relationship, and I keep it magnetized to our refrigerator door. A man sits at his desk, surrounded by calculator, notebook, scratch pad, and coffee, the telephone crooked to one ear, saying, "Right, you've got it. You're my best friend, my lover, *and* my wife. Now I've got to get off the phone and get this finished."

Or, as Rafe usually says on hanging up, "Keep in touch."

7

... AND
UNCOUPLING

The suburban homesteaders I know best are living two by two—and all of them sanctified by God, or at least the law. Which is why I naturally assumed, when a friend called me every Wednesday morning about 8:30, right after our children had left for elementary school, that she really had a weekly doctor's appointment.

"Hi," she'd say cheerily. "Can you keep an eye on my kids this afternoon? It's my shrink day."

One Wednesday I wasn't available for day care. "I'll be around tomorrow," I offered. "Can you change your appointment?"

Well, it turned out that it wasn't a psychiatrist at all that was getting her on the 11:06 every Wednesday morning. It was a Full Blooming Affair, she confided. It may or may not have been her first, but it certainly was mine. An affair—and right in the neighborhood!

The morality of the liaison didn't concern me—that was her business. What intrigued me was its management. (That, of course, was also her business.) This was a perfectly innocent affair, my neighbor assured me, a playful harmless dalliance. Just look at the circumstances: First of all, she said, he, too, was married, and both of them planned to stay that way. Second, he was prominent in civic affairs, so they *had* to be discreet. And finally, he had the use of an apartment every Wednesday afternoon. No tacky motels for them.

So much innocent fun was surely the stuff of romantic comedies, and every Wednesday afternoon as I put out milk and cookies for the neighborhood children, I fantasized a playlet of my own. With a nod to Noël Coward, I called it *Private Lives, American Style.*

Scene: A handsome sunlit aerie, with walls of books framing wide windows. At stage center a plump kid-upholstered sofa and a glass-and-chrome coffee table with fresh flowers in one crystal pitcher, martinis in another. The bright sun catches glints of plate glass, chrome, crystal, even of an aroused East River through the window at stage rear. At stage left, the door to the bedroom is ajar. The room is filled with the sweet spare sound of Pachelbel, or perhaps Palestrina.

When the curtain rises it is just past noon. The doorbell rings. Married Man puts out his cigarette and hurries stage right to greet Suburban Lady.

MM: Darling, do come in.

(SL steps in. She is very pretty and blond, and smartly dressed in traveling clothes. She walks to stage rear, stretches her arms wide with a little sigh of satisfaction, and regards the view with an ecstatic expression.)

SL: Heavenly! Look at that barge reflected in the river. Oh, darling, I am so happy.

MM (smiling): Are you?

SL: Aren't you?

MM: Of course I am. Tremendously happy.

SL: Just to think, here we are, you and I, not married! (She holds her face up to his.) Kiss me.

Scene fades. Blackout.

By the time the shadows fall on the trysting lovers, it is time for Gertie Lawrence to leave Noël Coward and ride the pumpkin coach back to suburbia and a spaghetti dinner. In the final frames, I see her sitting on the 4:43 among the other matinee ladies, the ones with their Playbills, a dreamy look in her eyes but guilt clutching her gut.

One day I played this short-short to my friend the Suburban Lady, and she burst out laughing.

"What actually happens is that I pick up a couple of deli sandwiches on my way to the apartment, and he picks up the beer. Sometimes a bottle of wine. Your offstage bedroom is a convertible couch in the studio-apartment, and our view is the Pearl-Wick Hampers sign in Long Island City. After a couple of hours, he has to rush back to his office and I have to clean the place up.

"What's more, not even a pang of guilt. If I have any guilt at all, it's because I don't have any guilt at all. We're having a great time, and we're not hurting anyone."

A few short months later those last words turned proverbially famous. He moved to a small bachelor pad in a nearby town, and she started to take care of her own kids on Wednesday afternoons. They hadn't been as discreet as they thought.

At about this time I was working on a project for a philan-thropic organization of which Married Man was a trustee. The night of one of the monthly board meetings MM, who had left his car as well as his wife back at the old homestead, asked me to give him a lift. When I rang the bell of his apartment, MM said, "I just got home from the office. I'm starving. Let's get a pizza and stay here for the evening."

After the board meeting I hurried home to tell Rafe the aston-ishing news of my first adulterous invitation. He was furious. Not that a man had found me attractive or adult enough for a little adultery, but that a man who knew *him* should be so perfidious, no matter how slight the acquaintance. Clearly, the unadulterated af-front was to my husband; I was merely the vehicle for it. As for me, I figured that here was a man who likes to amortize every empty apartment, or was taking Mae West's advice that "sex is like a small business; you gotta watch over it." And oh, yes, I was a little flat-tered.

Ordinarily I don't have a front-row seat at an assignation, close-focus lens in hand. More often, I'm totally ignorant of furtive cou-plings until I meet a friend in the supermarket, and as our carts clog the produce aisle, she says, "Boy! Did you hear . . .!" When I finally spot the mating couple, I do a double take, zoom in and sniff, "Hmmmph. What does he see in her?"

This is not a question I expect answered. He is always a middle-aged contemporary. She is usually a willowy twenty-five-year-old. Her hair is almost always long and straight, parted in the center, sometimes blond but more often brunette. She cannot play tennis, converse with the wisdom and wit of experience, even cook his dinner. No wonder my friends and I want to know what he sees in her.

Our husbands, however, have no questions at all. They know exactly what he sees in her. What's more, they know just what she sees in him. After all, he (like them) is attractively mellowed, with per-haps a touch of distinguishing gray around the temples/sideburns, has the wisdom and wit of experience, and is eager to teach her to play tennis.

My husband and his buddies weren't always this cool about December/May. The first time Rafe saw forty-nine-year-old Brian with his new young woman on the next tennis court, he double-faulted. The other three players couldn't keep the ball in play either. My God, they thought, What has Brian done to deserve *that!* Tiny, dark, and definitely not a tennis player, playing singles with Brian, a former club champion. And there was Brian, who doesn't voluntarily play with most of the A players, patiently explaining how to keep the wrist stiff, the eye on the ball, and follow through. The women playing on the far side of Brian, however, had absolutely no trouble keeping their eyes on the ball. Not for anything would they acknowledge the action on Brian's court. No comments at all—that is, not until they were cooling off and one of them muttered over the diet cola, "God, her mother is probably five years younger than Brian!"

By the time Brian's twenty-five-year-old friend had learned to serve, New Cookies, as Tom Wolfe dubbed them, had proliferated and were no longer unique at the tennis courts. The balance was shifting, and we Old Cookies knew with fear and trembling exactly in which direction. The acuteness of the tilt became apparent when I asked a long-divorced forty-six-year-old friend in public relations if he would like to meet a delightful woman I know who is thirty-eight.

"Oh, no, thanks," said Mr. PR. "Nothing over twenty-eight, please."

Ellen didn't have any such specifications in mind when she went back to graduate school. Ellen is forty-five and all she intended was to study psychology. Tim is twenty-seven. He was also studying psychology. They met in Ego Development and Character Disorder. Soon after, Ellen and Tim were having coffee after class in the college diner, talking about treatment modality, separation and in-dividuation, and psychodynamic formulation. It wasn't long before Ellen and Tim were having their coffee in Tim's apartment. There was never any question about Ellen leaving her husband and the affair ran its course as Psychology 311 ran *its* course. After the semester ended and Ellen and Tim went their separate ways, Ellen confided the extracurricular interlude to a good friend.

"But he's eighteen years younger!" wailed the friend. "How could you?"

"Easy," said Ellen. "It was like falling backward into a bowl of raspberries."

Tumbling inadvertently into forbidden fruit is the perfect image for the delicious romantic adventure that an affair seems to be to many of its mid-life participants. Guiltless in an age of permissiveness. Euphorically adolescent at middle age. Whatever other needs it meets—hostility toward a spouse, show of strength, asserting the emotional upper hand, reassurance of libidinous vitality, approval from a new friend—an extramarital affair guarantees at least a sip from the fountain of youth.

The restorative powers of an extramarital affair seem particularly compelling these days, to husbands and wives alike. Roger Gould suggests why. "The prevalence of sexual stimuli in the culture, the free-sex ethic, the decrease in our parental inhibitions, the emergence of our children's sexuality and our sudden sense of urgency all combine to form a very powerful push into extramarital sexuality," explains Gould. "We feel this is our last chance to explore new sexual or romantic territory. Soon we'll be fifty or sixty and our youth will be over—our bodies will be less attractive. . . . Since we no longer feel guilty about sex, we see it as our right to pursue new pleasures."

For most men, these new pleasures are more fruitfully pursued with younger women. "If we are to understand it better," writes Levinson of the December/May liaison, "we have to look at the extramarital relationship from a developmental perspective. It reflects a man's struggles with the Young/Old polarity: he is asserting his youthful vitality at a time when he fears that the Young in him is being crushed by the dry, dying Old. If he is seeking merely to recapture his adolescece, or to keep it fixed immutably, the search will be in vain."

These male Decembers expect their winsome young Mays to recall—better yet, restore—their peak performance, affirm their youthful virility, and appreciate their years of experience. These days, however, winsome young May is not as unknowing or inexperienced as December might expect, not necessarily bowled over by his sexual expertise. Indeed, she is likely to have a lot more know-how than the old man, which may threaten rather than affirm his sexuality. The traditional young-old, male-female configurations are in flux, and no one knows this better than the middle-aged woman.

The powerful push into adultery is felt even more strongly by mid-life wives who are pursuing their extramarital pleasures in ever greater numbers, at least according to *Cosmopolitan* magazine. A survey of 106,000 women, analyzed by Linda Wolfe, found that 54 percent of the married women were unfaithful, and that among wives over thirty-five the incidence rose to almost 70 percent. That seven out of ten wives are unfaithful doesn't surprise the mid-life women I know who work in offices; almost universally they report that young single men seem to enjoy the company of older women who, in turn, don't in the least mind being noticed, admired, flattered, and often bedded. (And more and more often wedded, according to Neugarten, who is amassing a file on older women who have married younger men. "The age difference is not the 30 or 40 years we see when the man is older," she reports, "but the stories comment on the way public attitudes are shifting.")

But what I hear from the few middle-aged wives who share their extramarital pleasures with the rest of us is that a young lover is definitely not a requisite. A man of any age can restore youthful rapture—as long as he is attentive, pleasant, and, let's face it, sexually competent. In fact, there can be definite drawbacks to a young lover, which came as some surprise to my friend Martha. Martha hangs around with filmmakers and other creative types, so the idea of younger men was not only definitely appealing but her lifestyle made them definitely available. Moreover, Martha knows that middle-aged women are usually running in finely tuned overdrive, while their male contemporaries are often slogging along in first or second—when they get in gear at all. As long as Martha was married and pursued her afternoon pleasures in a SoHo loft, the arrangement gave each participant pleasure. The problem came when Martha left her husband and moved to her own place.

"Naturally, I expected my friend to stay the night," she said. To the three other middle-aged ladies having lunch with Martha, it seemed a perfectly natural expectation. "He wouldn't stay over!" The recollection still infuriates her. "What's more, neither would the next one. They all have to go back to their own little beds! They're like little boys who don't have permission to have a sleep-over."

These younger men are much younger men—at least fifteen years her junior—and it occurred to me that perhaps the Oedipal relationship is not an equal opportunity taboo. It seems to encourage the older man—younger woman (i.e., father-daughter) relationship but inhibit the older woman–younger man (mother-son) coupling. The experience of another friend seems to corroborate the thesis.

Jean is forty-six years old, divorced, and confidently leading a newly independent life. She was walking home one day from work, thinking over the important things a man had told her about their just-terminated relationship. She stopped at her neighborhood pub for a glass of wine. It was the first time she had gone to a bar alone. A young man struck up a conversation. They spent a lovely hour talking. He walked her home. As he left her at the front door, they made a date for dinner the following night.

Dinner was fun, again the conversation was bright and interesting. He walked her home. This time he said, "Well? What do you think?"

"How old are you?" asked Jean.

"Thirty-three," the young man answered.

"I can't," she sighed. "You're just too young."

"I understand," said the young man. And she thinks he did. "If you ever change your mind, here's my number."

She still has his number. She hasn't called it.

"Is it because you have a twenty-four-year-old son?" I ask her.

"Maybe," she answers slowly. "I just didn't feel comfortable about it. The age difference seemed *huge.*"

Once in a while the age difference even seems huge to a male December, and when one of us mid-life wives knows such a man, we pass along his heartening story to all our contemporaries (male and female), spreading the tale of his fall and rise as if it held magical restorative powers. As indeed it does. Max was one such man, and

I don't remember exactly whose friend he is, but there are many of us who hold him dear. Just after his divorce, forty-nine-year-old Max took out a succession of young nubiles; eventually they palled. "All they wanted to do was talk about Ingmar Bergman," he complained, "and I'd already *talked* about Bergman. With my wife. When we were both young." Next Thanksgiving Max is marrying a forty-nine-year-old divorcée, and the grapevine reports they are both gloriously happy.

Larry is another such man with a similar tale. In the course of one year, poor confused Larry underwent the kind of emotional slalom that developmental psychologists frequently chronicle in mid-life men. The event that triggered Larry's mid-life panic was the heart attack of a friend in the middle of a Manhattan street. His friend survived, but the episode traumatized Larry. Mortality was much too close. Larry took the popular preventive medicine: an alluring young woman. Their relationship became serious. Larry divorced his wife and married alluring May.

Larry settled down in his romantic new nest, and all was blissful for several months. They biked the city streets together on weekends, hung out at coffee shops at night with May's young friends. They brunched every Sunday at a different trendy café, and some Sundays, Larry later recalled, he ended up hosting such a crowd of young people that it reminded him of visiting his son at college and taking out half the dorm for lunch. If youth was what Larry was after, he certainly fell into it. He was also embarrassingly typical of the mid-life man Levinson describes as "so anxious about aging and dying that he denies these concerns altogether and attempts to remain the perpetual Young . . .who insists on remaining youthful in the early adult sense, trying to have now the good times that he earlier missed."

Then May wanted to have a baby. Another family was the last thing Larry wanted. He had already brought up one family. He wanted to be young, not have young. Little things started to annoy him. Her friends were always dropping in. There was never enough privacy. It was too noisy. Didn't she know he had to get up early in the morning for work, for God's sake?

Meanwhile, his first wife had struck out for the West Coast to make a new life for herself. At the end of the year she came east to discuss mutual business matters.

"Say," ventured Larry, "are you happy?"

"Not really. You?"

"Not terribly."

Yes, Larry divorced May and remarried Mrs. Larry. A happy December/December finale to those of us who follow mid-life's comic operettas. But it was more than a victory for the middle-aged sisterhood. It was, in a sense, a validation of maturity, an affirmation of appropriateness, an acceptance of oneself. Of all the ways we thrash around in our mid-life agonies, of all the routes we take out of our mid-life *angst*—and they seem to focus on mortality, age, vulnerability—what the lessons of Max and Larry may be telling us is that fleeing back to what was, or to what might have been, is not necessarily the road forward, that crossing the generational boundaries simply doesn't work.

Daniel Levinson observed, "At mid-life a man may have much contact with persons in their 20s and 30s, but he cannot participate as a full peer in their world . . . he must offer them something distinctive that reflects his greater maturity, his membership in the generation of middle adulthood. . . . If he remains too tied to young adults, he will be isolated from his own generation and split off from the Old in himself, and he may lose all generational ties."

Whether or not he is bolting his own generation, or simply seeking contemporary alternatives, most of the time, you will have noticed, it is the husband who wanders off the reservation, leaving his Old Cookie to crumble. Once in a while, a wife says she's had enough of a bad marriage, and the local sisterhood rejoices. We hope not only that she will find her way with dignity and success and fun, but also that he will be unbearably lonely, eat canned tuna fish every night, and spend Saturdays taking his dirty shirts to the laundry. It doesn't always work out that way.

Take Pete and Edie. About the time that Edie marked her fortieth birthday, it occurred to her that Pete was no longer very interesting. He was becoming positively obsessed with his sports, she complained. Out playing them all weekend. Up watching them on the tube every night. He simply hadn't grown with her, she said, confirming what Gould tells us is a classic mid-life marriage pattern (although most of the time we hear about husbands who have outgrown their wives). While the rest of us marked our fortieth birthdays with bifocals, Edie took herself to a two-day seminar in self-actualization and came home fully centered and in touch with all of her feelings, most of them hostile. Pete would please leave the house as soon as possible so she could launch her new life of creative independence. Regretfully, Pete moved out of the comfortable Victorian house and into a small sterile studio apartment with his big TV set. A little nervously he began a bachelor life for the second time. He needn't have worried. From the first night he was besieged with invitations. Movies. Dinners. Picnics. Bridge games. "Please," he begged his friends, "at least let me stay home and watch Monday night football."

Of course, the most satisfactory separations are those by mutual consent. The couples who still like and respect each other but just don't want to hang their toothbrushes side by side any longer. We are blessed with two friends whose divorce and subsequent friendship is so civil they shame many a marriage.

When Jane and Mort decided to split, they rented a house in London for a month and took their four children on a holiday. After a lot of familial love and laughs over the Dover sole and Devon cream, Jane and Mort called the children into the paneled living room on the last day to break the news. I don't know if the elegant Belgravia setting made the separation any easier to take, but the children did come home with a strong sense of family.

Jane and Mort live near each other, and the children move freely between the two homes. They frequently have lunch or dinner together, talk over family problems, and share a good many other thoughts as well. Freed from the abrading resentments and hostilities that made their marriage so gritty, they seem to be better friends now than before. Because Jane and Mort wanted their divorce equally, because neither felt ill used by the other, they value the past that they shared for so many years. Equally important, they understand that they don't have a future together. In those circumstances, Gould tells us, "both partners usually consider the divorce a marvelous release. Even if they never remarry, they are free to pursue a new life more suited to the selves they are at mid-life."

Jane promptly started her own business and wrote her first book. Mort embarked on the series of romantic entanglements an early marriage had foreclosed. Independently they were doing what they couldn't do together.

"Mort is a dear, dear friend of mine," says Jane.

"Jane is a terrific person," says Mort. "There's nothing I wouldn't do for her." As Gould observes, "Once we resolve the guilt and blame and work through the anger, ex-spouses can make valuable friends. After all, who knows us better?"

By the time Mort had stabilized with twenty-six-year-old Karen, Jane was cooking holiday turkey for Mort and his lady friend, and they were inviting her to join their ski weekends. And when Karen wanted to surprise Mort on his fiftieth birthday, she planned a cocktail party and called Jane for the forties and fifties part of the guest list. (When December plans a party for May, it is likely to take place in a disco, as some of my friends are starting to find out.)

"How did you enjoy the party?" I asked Jane.

"It was really nice to see all our old friends—and were they surprised to see me there! And it was wonderful to see the surprise and pleasure on Mort's face when he arrived. I was completely comfortable with all of that. The only thing that was weird is that Karen and her friends are *hundreds* of years younger than I am."

That was precisely the age difference I felt when Rafe and I spent a summer weekend with Mort and Karen at the beach. I'll skip over the string bikini and the long-wet-hair-droplets-of-water-on-bronzed-skin nymphet look. I'll even skip over the unnerving discovery that it is possible for twenty-six to make wise and witty conversation. What pointed up the age difference so acutely was the schedule of events. When we were ready for breakfast, they were still abed. We all met at the midday meal, it being our lunch and their breakfast. Our postbeach, late-afternoon nap was over by seven, and we were ready for dinner at eight-thirty, which we thought a civilized time for dining. They didn't finish napping, or whatever, until nine-thirty, and for them dinner before ten or eleven was unthinkable. Then came the postmidnight walk on the sand, and more whatever. It's no surprise that when Mort occasionally runs into Rafe in the city, he confides that sometimes he doesn't think he can meet all the demands made on him. On those occasions, reports Rafe when he gets home, "Can you imagine. Four times a night, at his age!"

I'm not sure if he's envious or relieved.

8

BODY WORKS
AND THE
SPORTING LIFE

Four-times-a-night Mort can't be any more exhausted than his middle-aged siblings who are Exercycling to the "Today" show, pumping iron at lunchtime, and jogging after work. Whether tumbling on the Beautyrest or working out on the exercise mat, we are all after the same thing: confirmation that we still are as we were. Or that we soon will be again. To psychoanalyst and sociology professor Dr. Elliott Jaques, sexual promiscuity and obsession over health and appearance are just different routes to the same end: not growing old. "The entry upon the psychological scene of the reality and inevitability of one's own eventual personal death is the central and crucial feature of the mid-life phase," he writes.

In the current mania for fitness, a compelling catalyst, at least among the middle-aged, is the press of mortality. Mid-life joggers may believe they are circling the track for cardiovascular fitness; they are also running like hell for their lives. We seem to have a magical belief (fervent hope is probably more accurate) that if we move fast and faithfully enough, we can outrun the grim reaper. One fiftyish woman I know who by profession is a clear-headed researcher, says, "If I swim my forty-four laps a day, I know I will live forever."

Making an ally of one's body is surely one good way to cope with mortality. And, God knows, the impetus is there. Most mid-lifers feel betrayed by their bodies. The flesh sags, the hair recedes and/or grays, the joints swell. It is small comfort to know that actually one's physical capacities have been gradually sliding downhill since age thirty.

For most people, the discovery of the body's betrayal occurs ten or fifteen years later, and it usually shocks like a thunderbolt. Especially men. Classically, it happens on a sunny day when a younger man beats his middle-aged opponent at some sport. It's worse yet when the younger man is his son. In our own family, David was twelve when he took his first set of tennis off his father (who is nowhere near as incompetent a player as the event would suggest). It turned out to be a blessing in disguise; David was so young and so talented with his racquet that the old man didn't suffer as he might have at the hands of an older child. It was rather like having a hysterectomy at thirty; you don't mistake it for menopause. Nevertheless, the fatherly good sportsmanship was a bit moderated at the dinner table that night for, after all, as Levinson points out, "A man at mid-life is suffering some loss of his youthful vitality and often, some insult to his youthful narcissistic pride."

There is also no dodging the notion that sports are a compelling male metaphor. In his study of mid-life men, Levinson found that "many had a lifelong interest, as participants and spectators, in competitive sports such as football, basketball, and boxing. It was hard to say whether they were more attracted by the competitive aspect or by the bodily skill, endurance and power."

Some years ago I witnessed an impressive example of Levinson's thesis. Two men were cooling off in a swimming pool after a singles match. The poolside spectators gradually became aware that the competition had simply changed venues. The two male bodies were racing; now the test was underwater laps. The crazed performance electrified the spectators. The male onlookers seemed embarrassed to witness such a raw display of competition; the women mentally ran through their pulmonary resuscitation first aid. The interesting thing is that nobody seemed surprised, least of all the two wives.

The fellow who issued the swimming challenge (and who had obviously lost the tennis match) is the same fellow who, six months later, wouldn't get off the slopes after his ski bindings broke. His middle-aged bones splintered in six places and were slow to heal, so the following tennis season he hopped, broken leg and all, onto the court on crutches to play one-legged singles. Not playing was not one of his options. No wonder Levinson found that ". . . associated with manliness is bodily prowess and toughness—the stamina to. . . endure severe bodily stress without 'quitting.'"

Men don't have to push to the very limits of endurance to act out their manly prowess. Instead, they can rely on the "performance factor" of themselves or of the team they have invested with the magic. I may (or may not) be the only wife whose marriage depends on how successful the New York Giants are, or how well Himself executes a backhand. I am certainly not the only wife to irritate her husband merely by being his tennis partner. I use the term advisedly. I am never in any sense a real partner; at best I am the silent partner. When we play mixed doubles, he covers the center court and I get the alley. I am rarely allowed within the singles lines, but I do have a territory all my own. It's about three feet wide and two feet deep, measured from the net, and he's very decent about my autonomy within it. He won't poach on my space as long as I don't invade his. When he misses a shot that would ordinarily be on my half of the court, he yells, "Well, couldn't you move just a little?" He finds it barely acceptable that every four games the rules require that I actually set foot on his turf to serve.

The reason we are fundamentally at odds as a doubles team (I refuse to contemplate the larger ramifications of that) is that we have fundamentally divergent approaches to the game. I would rather play well and lose than be a sloppy winner. I don't care if I get a bad line call; I figure that if I really deserved the point, I can make it again. Who needs a partner like this? If Rafe could manage to forgive the lack of killer instinct, there is still the unforgivable sin: I don't take it seriously enough. Like most women, I don't appreciate the central meaning that sports has for many men. "Playing sports after work, or watching sports on TV, is a serious matter for many men," Levinson notes.

Sometimes it's even a serious matter before work. This is the case with a local early morning tennis group. This is not just four men who get up before dawn to play tennis, then rush home to shower and make the 8:02 to the office. This is a club. It has rules. It has members. It may even have exclusionary membership policies, since I note the roster of eighteen to twenty members each year is always male. This is a formal and resolute association of racquet-wielding colleagues. It has an acronym—actually two, depending on the season and the game. From the first week in May to the first week in October the group is known as INERTA (International Early

Regular Tennis Association); the rest of the year it is called INEPTA (International Early Paddle, etcetera). It has a logo (racquet player rampant) and a motto ("Don't Muff It").

All year long the same set of strictly enforced bylaws pertain. These cover starting time ("6:45 A.M. *sharp*"); weather conditions for play ("When in doubt, show up"); substitutes; fair play ("All shots are to be considered in, unless a player clearly sees a shot to be out"); and attendance requirements. This last rule is strictly enforced. One member who failed to show for his scheduled game was served a disciplinary complaint; a second infraction is cause for summary expulsion. It was a lesson well taken by other club members. One fellow, whose business was keeping him in Germany longer than expected, called his wife frantically. Did he ask about the children? Did he inquire about his wife? The agitated message was: "For God's sake, be sure and get me a replacement for the game." My friend Jim, who is founder and chief executive officer of the club, remembers well the call he received from a conscientious member delayed in California. The member (obviously functioning without his secretary) called Jim at 3:00 A.M., thinking that when he placed the call at midnight, it was a respectable 9:00 P.M. in the East.

The middle-aged jocks who require this early morning sporting event to remind them they are still twenty-six years old arise before six summer and winter. In the summer, six can be the start of a cool and lovely dawn. In winter, it is still night, cold and dark. They get dressed in the dark (if they know what's good for them, say the wives), and they play under lights. By the time they return home to shower, the wives may or may not have recovered their good nature. At the First (and only) Annual Awards Dinner, which did include women, there was a Wife of the Year Award for early-morning cheerfulness and breakfast-making. No one qualified.

As they drive to the courts, these predawn racqueteers are likely to pass any number of solitary joggers whose daily runs are stayed neither by wind nor rain, sleet nor snow. As often as not, they are in training for some race or other. I almost said marathon, but, as a seventy-two-year-old runner recently rebuked me, "People are always calling any three- or five- or ten-mile race a marathon. A marathon," he sniffed, "is twenty-six miles and three hundred and eighty-five yards."

My friend Nancy doesn't need any such instruction; she knows precisely how long a marathon is. She started running three years ago and, last week, just shy of her fifty-fourth birthday, she had a moment of ecstasy in the local half-marathon. "It was mind-blowing to find I could run at the same pace and distance with twenty-year-old men who are in superb physical shape. Mind-blowing." The last time she ran competitively she finished first in the over-fifty category, and her time was faster than the over-forty winner. "Even though my eyesight is getting worse, and my hearing is suspect, it's exhilarating to be reminded that when pressed, our bodies as a whole can deliver. It's a wonderful, liberating feeling. The step is livelier. You feel younger." She hesitated. "It's not exactly that you feel younger. You feel *able*."

Well, not everybody feels able, but everybody sure as hell is trying. When Nancy began running three years ago, she ran on weekends with two friends. Pretty soon they brought their spouses, and before they could towel off, it was a jogging club. Seven or eight or ten couples meeting every Sunday morning at a different house. Some of them run (about seven miles is par) and some of them walk (a mile or so). The host maps out the routes through his neighborhood and provides that week's brunch at the finish line. Sometimes Rafe and I are invited for the Danish and coffee, even though we haven't sweated out our dues on the course.

The recent popularity of walking is still a surprise to my suburban eyes. City folk walk all over, but where I live, the only pedestrians were on their way to the service station to retrieve their cars (and then only because no one was around to give them a lift). It wasn't literally true that you would be picked up for loitering, but you might well be stopped by a passing patrol car and asked what your business was. Now, of course, people are striding purposefully all along suburban roads and the main problem in our mostly sidewalk-less village is how to avoid getting hit by a car.

The reason I know that walking is a certifiably popular sport is that I have recently taken it up. Never at the cutting edge (the cusp, I think it's now called) of fashion, I am a reliable indicator of the mainstream. When Rafe and I visited friends in San Francisco and I found myself hiking five miles around Angel Island when I could have been sampling Chardonnay in the Napa Valley, I knew something was afoot. So I wasn't surprised when our friends, who last year lazed on a beach, for two weeks, are backpacking in Olympic National Park this year, or that another couple, who plied the restaurant route in France last year, are hiking in Maine this year.

Using the same litmus test on myself, you can be sure that long-distance swimming is in. At the public pools where I keep wet, serious swimmers think nothing of doing a seventy-one-lap mile daily. Serious swimmers feel they must swim the crawl. Serious swimmers feel they must swim continuously; no resting between laps. Serious swimmers feel that the clock stops when they stop. Then there are the more frivolous who, for want of a better description, can be called the Poky Paddlers. Any stroke that propels us to the opposite end of the pool, at any speed whatsoever, qualifies. We are so pleased with our progress that we often celebrate our arrival there by stopping to enjoy the water view. If we could get away with it, we would keep a cumulative tally of our laps from the very first swim of the year.

Health seekers know that swimming is a cardiovascular activity par excellence. Body-beautiful seekers know that it is a relatively painless way to exercise; you don't get golf or tennis elbow, shin splints, or even overheated. The worst of it is you have to get wet. And as Frank, our local spa master, unwittingly pointed out when he was trying to sell me a membership, "Who needs swimming? Swimming exercises all your muscles at once. On our machines you can do them one by one."

Despite Frank's convoluted logic, he did indeed manage to sell me a spa membership one year that introduced me to the intimate, self-indulgent, narcissistic world of body culture. I matriculated as a functional illiterate in hot tubs, lufa mitts, and lat pulls, but by the time I graduated—barely—I understood the relationship between the bench press and a sleek, well-turned chassis. And I knew just how far these body shops go to meet our mid-life longings.

No question about it. The exercise emporia are our fantasy factories. Call them spas, health management centers, even give them quasi-medical status as cardio-fitness institutes, fundamentally they are the temples where we lift our mid-life prayers for health, beauty, and of course, youth. They are the palaces where men can tune up their maleness and women tone up their femaleness.

Men and women go for different but parallel reasons. As Levinson wrote of the masculine patterns in mid-life: "If [a man's] body is a vehicle for demonstrating his masculinity, he tries to acquire special strength, endurance, sexual virility, athletic prowess." What better place than the local health spa? With Levinson as a model, we can project similar motivations for women: If a woman's body is a vehicle for demonstrating her femininity, she tries to acquire shapeliness and sexual allure. What better place than the local health spa?

Second only to youth (i.e., virility for men, beauty for women) as a motivating force is health. If a man hasn't already found his way to a health center, the regimen will occur to him as soon as he, or a peer, suffers an illness. The minute word came down from the ski slopes that our friend Ben had suffered a heart attack, the applications began to roll in at the local cardio-fitness center where, ironically, Ben had faithfully put in his time. Even while Ben was recuperating he proselytized for it. "Join it," he'd urge his friends. "The doctors said that if I hadn't worked out there, I'd be dead."

Any illness has a profound effect on both men and women in middle age, but the impact is subtly different. "Health changes are more of an age marker for men than for women," explains Bernice Neugarten. "Women are more concerned over the body-monitoring of their husbands than of themselves." I have seen this syndrome at work in my parents' bedroom where, for the last fifteen years, my (healthy) wakeful mother keeps one eye on my (healthy) sleeping father all night to be sure that he hasn't stopped breathing. So when my friend Maggie gave her husband a membership in the cardio-fitness center for his forty-eighth birthday, I understood her generosity. At the bottom of our concern for our husbands' health is our fear for ourselves, our dread of being widowed. We are acting out what Neugarten calls "rehearsal for widowhood." If (when) that terrifying event occurs, at least we'd better be in shape for it: sleek, taut, and as young as possible. So for very different but related reasons men and women work out their needs at the body shops.

Questing after my own private dream ("Inside the Body You Have Is The Body You've Always Wanted" was the way the spa brochure put it), I found the local health spa a serviceable microcosm of the genre. Take its physical appearance. A flattened orb perched like a top on a concrete shaft, it hovers over a wide commercial strip like a spaceship that has escaped from a screen of the Quad 1-2-3-4 a mile south and has not quite touched down.

Inside the large circular exercise room is a chrome jungle. Rollers for hips and rollers for thighs, stationary jogging tracks and bicycles, slant boards and knee curlers, body presses and leg presses, bars and pulleys and weights, weights, weights. Practically the only motorized appliance is something called a spiralator. You rest your upper torso, back arched, on the stationary top section, grab the hand rails over your head, and hang on for dear life while the bottom section relentlessly rotates hips and legs. Despite its superficial resemblance to a medieval torture rack, the spiralator is marvelously relaxing.

Likewise the whirlpool where jet streams of 108° water pummel knotted muscles from every direction. Giving oneself to this wet massage, it is all too easy to understand how California hot tubbers can be lulled into euphoria and eventual oblivion. (At the spa the antidote to such death by boiling is the cold plunge into three feet of 50° water, which shocks you into a different mode of insensibility.)

The restorative powers of thermal baths and plunges have been known to many ancient civilizations but it was the Romans who perfected the adornment of public baths, so it was to the Romans that the spa decorators naturally turned. Here in the whirlpool room, for example, is a wraparound mosaic with a full complement of classical figures and symbols: a bare-breasted female warrior subduing a naked man on his knees; a fig-leafed male reining in two rearing white horses; another wrestling with a bull; a seven-headed snake, its seven red tongues spitting. And like the Roman baths, men and women do not use the spa facilities simultaneously (except for a few communal hours every Sunday afternoon).

Fantasies truly flower every Friday at eleven o'clock when belly dancing is on the spa curriculum. Baledi Dancing, Egyptian-style. The staff swears it's as good for the body as the gymnastic exercises, and very few women need convincing. To the strains of "Egyptian Nights," serious belly dancers put on their finger cymbals and don their hip belts jangling with rows of chained coins. I don't know if it's sociologically significant that the two most elaborately outfitted women are the oldest and the heaviest in the class.

When I report to my friend Marie that it is not at all easy to keep your back straight and gyrate properly, Marie groans. "If only they had taught us belly dancing at college, I would have passed posture pictures sooner." Marie and I went to the same New England woman's school and it had only one firm requirement for graduation: a perfect posture picture. I had no idea before I went there that proper carriage was central to a woman's education. It took some of us four years of exercises to correct our offending S-curves or slouches and, despite mitigating circumstances like academic honors, qualify for our sheepskins.

Whether gyrating to "Egyptian Nights" or relaxing in a semicircular cubbyhole in the whirlpool's steaming caldron or pumping iron on the leg press, one senses a communal underlay to the earnest body work. Here is our modern forum. Here information is exchanged, rumors generated, issues examined.

Item: On one bike a black leotard with a throaty cultivated voice and teased blond hair: "My third trip to Spain, and I won't go to Europe again to be treated like a second-class citizen. Nevuhtheless, it's interesting to see other cultures, and the Roman ruins around Sebilla and Cordoba." She pronounces the towns with a Castilian accent.

On the next Schwinn, a swarthy young woman: "You can go to the South Bronx for the ruins—and you'll see a different culture there, too."

Item: On neighboring slant boards, firming up the abdominals, a perky new young member to a middle-aged woman who is eying the butterfly tattoo over her right breast fluttering out over the low-cut leotard: "I have another one," says Lydia the taaaatooooed lady. "A moon and a star," she says, patting her left hipbone. "It isn't as cute now as I thought it was when I was sixteen."

Item: On the bench press, maroon leotard rhythmically pushing 30-pound weights up and down ("Exhale up, inhale down"): "As soon as you stop doing your exercises, everything spreads." As my friend Jamie said after calling the plumber for the third time in a month, "Ninety percent of life is maintenance."

Item: In the steam room, two middle-aged bodies rubbing off their dried skin with lufa mitts, like reptiles shedding a former life.

"What's your birthday?"

"July thirteenth."

"Oh, you're a Cancer. What's your husband?"

"He's a Pisces."

"Pisces are pretty impotent."

"Boy! You can say that again."

The whirlpool complex, with the Eucalyptus Room, the steam room, sauna and sun room, is the R and R of the spa regimen. After working up a sweat, this is where you recuperate and fantasize. There are always loungers in plastic chaises surveying the whirlpool as if it were the surf at Miami Beach, tilting their faces heavenward, evidently expecting the sun to peek through the asbestos tile ceiling. Here the body talk often centers on finishing touches: face lifts by surgery, face lifts by acupuncture, face lifts by invisible masking tape, massages, varicose veins. Massages I've discussed with a friend who goes to the Y every Wednesday morning for yoga and a massage. Yoga is tranquillity and exercise, massage is Mrs. Johnson, a woman from Alabama with a well-defined philosophy of her trade. "Don't worry, honey," she says, pounding away. "We'll just make these fat cells so soft you can move them around anywhere you like."

Varicose veins I've discussed with another friend. She is forty-seven. She has had varicose veins since she was eighteen. Nevertheless, it is now imperative that they be corrected. At once. She cannot wait out another season. No matter that at a business convention last week a woman asked her if she was her husband's second (read younger) wife. (She is not; they are even the same age.) Or that at another office party one secretary saw her with her husband and said, "I didn't know Sam's daughter worked here, too."

None of this consoles her in the least. The problem, as I see it, is not varicose veins at all. It is, what will she do next month when the varicose veins are gone? She'll still be forty-seven.

This is a problem I know only too well. One bleak February day when a particularly long and hard northeastern winter had chilled even the warmest good nature, my pals Stella and Judith suggested we seek refuge and restoration in one of those sybaritic palaces where one is pampered from topknot to toenail. And so we threw ourselves into our virgin adventure with Swedish masseuses, soothing herbal wraps, steaming facials, Scotch douches (this is not what you think), and, as a finale, elaborate makeup to gild us pale lilies. We left the plush premises massaged and rouged to a rosy glow, giggling like adolescents dressed for a first prom, to meet our husbands for dinner. They didn't notice a thing. And the next morning, after the eyeliner had smudged, the cheekbone enhancer had washed off, and the wrinkle eraser had erased itself, there we were, still three middle-aged ladies, not a day younger and a good deal poorer.

9

WHITE WATER AND OTHER MIDSTREAM GAMBOLS

Shortly after a new principal came to our high school, he mentioned a course he wished he could institute: Risk Taking. "But, of course, we'd have to guarantee a passing grade or no one would take it," he said, grinning.

He knows his customers. Most of the middle-class students he oversees are not gamblers. They sign up for "safe" traditional courses rather than venture into unknown and perhaps more challenging areas. They operate on the need-to-know theory: If I don't need it for college, I don't need it.

Moreover, they don't just want to pass a course, they want to pass it well. They want to establish their place in the pecking order. When the school offered them a pass/fail grading system several years ago, they all said, No way. Not for them a simple pass or fail. How will Yale or Boston University or Michigan be able to distinguish their A-quality pass from their classmate's C-quality pass? What they'd really like is an even more finely tuned and differentiated grading system so they could edge out their classmate's 91.3 with their own 91.4.

What an ironic turn. Here we have our presumably laid-back youth needing encouragement to take chances, to gamble. At the same time, their mid-life elders, who might understandably be slowing down, sliding into complacency, seem to be turning more and more from safely guaranteed paths to put themselves at risk in various ways.

Actually, there is a direct and fascinating developmental relationship between the cautious self-protecting child and the risk-taking adult, according to Roger Gould. "We must risk doing something foolish for a change," he believes. "For only then can we accept the idea that in childhood (or as adults in the grip of childhood consciousness), we were so afraid of demonic fathers that we endured whatever treatment came our way and didn't explore options in life." Shucking off our childhood fears is a way to gain mastery over our lives. "As adults we can replace the illusion of parental protection; we can take calculated risks in order to be free."

By calculated risks, I don't think Gould means the kind of foolhardy bravado I can usually count on from my father. He is eighty-five years old and fiercely independent. He runs after buses as they pull away from the curb, rushes into traffic to find a taxi. He still believes the "vague promise" Gail Sheehy described in *Passages,* "that by becoming masters of their own destiny they will beat even the grim reaper." When he and my mother were accosted one evening by two muggers, my mother screamed and my father pushed them away with his umbrella.

"Lucky for you they ran away," I said.

"Lucky nothing," he answered testily. "Who did they think they were!"

No, the jeopardy I'm talking about is not adrenalized gut reaction, even in defiance of danger. It's a more contemplative act, requiring the taker to acknowledge the hazard. It requires careful thought, assessment of the gamble, and then a measured choice. It stretches limits, seeks outposts in unfamiliar terrain. It is fueled by restlessness, by mid-life *angst,* by the uneasy apprehension of deadlines closing in, of some vague yet insistent beat of "now or never." "There is the sense of the last chance," says Rosenbaum. "We confront habit and boredom. We see aging in our partners." Always there is urgency, the feeling that time is short, or at least finite. As Neugarten points out, we are beginning to perceive time in a different way. "Life is restructured in terms of time left to live rather than time since birth." Observes Gould: "The desire for stability and continuity which characterized our thirties is being replaced by a relentless inner demand for action."

Action for what? For the lost dreams, the paths not taken, the might-have-beens. Levinson eloquently describes the energizing factor: "Internal voices that have been muted for years now clamor to be heard . . . grief over lost opportunities, outrage over betrayal by others, guilt over betrayal by oneself . . . an identity prematurely rejected, or a love lost or not pursued; . . . an internal figure who wants to be an athlete or nomad or artist, to marry for love or remain a bachelor, to get rich or enter the clergy or live a sensual carefree life—possibilities set aside earlier to become what he now is."

Sometimes our internal voices call up dramatic changes and high risks. Emotionally, intellectually, sexually, physically. Sometimes the risks look small, sometimes foolish to others, but to the risk taker the perils are real. And necessary. "It is only by risking our persons from one hour to another that we live at all," wrote William James. It seems to be a noticeable mid-life condition.

I hesitate to draw conclusions just because I find myself clipping information on what to carry on mountain climbs, how to behave at high altitudes, and looking up alien terms like hyperventilation. This is particularly outlandish if you consider that we are not partial to heights and that our idea of a splendid vacation is a tennis court at sea level, and gin and tonics on demand. So what prompted Rafe and me to rise at 5:00 A.M. and hike ten miles through rough and dangerous terrain stalking rhino when we could have sensibly made the same hunt in a comfortable zebra-striped van like most other people? Scientific inquiry doesn't flourish by extrapolating from one's own curious behavior. But I do notice, for instance, that many people I know are taking very different vacations from the ones they used to.

Consider my friend Pam, who for forty-seven years would only travel by surface transportation. She just flew, white knuckles and all, to Peru, where, to heighten the adventure, she was obliged to hike up to Machu Picchu when the roads washed out, gasping for breath in the high altitude.

"What made you do it after all these years?" I ask.

"If not now, when?"

Or take my friend Kate, a soft-spoken, gentle librarian who by her own admission is not adventurous. "I don't have a lot of courage" is how she put it. But there was Kate, hanging onto a rubber raft, awash in glacially cold white water in a turbulent Pacific Northwest river. "After five or six times of careening headlong toward huge rocks, I began to trust the oarsman," she reports. "It really wasn't so bad." She pauses. "Actually, I was so proud of myself when it was over."

What made her go in the first place? Not a conscious choice, to be sure. She was accompanying her husband at his business convention, and the outing was planned for the group. But still, she could have refused. Visited the Seattle Art Museum. Pleaded a headache.

Then there is Carol. "You should have seen me," she exulted on her return from one vacation. "I went up in a balloon! I couldn't believe myself. When I was a kid I wouldn't even go on a donkey down into the Grand Canyon." This year she is flying through the Grand Canyon in a bush plane after a white-water trip on the Colorado River. What's more, she has already given me instructions about the slide show I am to present at her funeral. This future eulogy is to be a pictorial odyssey of her moments of triumph: hovering over the landscape in the balloon gondola, bush flying in Arizona, and maybe, by that time, even hang gliding and rappeling.

And then, of course, there is John. John positively exemplifies the mid-life risk taker. John is a New York lawyer. He likes politics and paddle tennis. He has a wife and six children. They are all active in church and community affairs. None of this prepared his friends —not to mention his family—for John's adventure at the age of fifty-five: crossing the Atlantic in a forty-foot sailboat.

To begin with, John was a novice sailor when his friend, another novice, invited him to join the crew. "I knew it was dangerous," says John. "But it was an adventure, a chance of a lifetime that few people ever get." Moreover, he had his adventure in full measure: Force-10 hurricane winds, forty-foot waves, the loss of the auxiliary engine, the radio transmitter, and seven of their nine sails before the boat reached Ireland twenty-six days later.

"I'm a different person, a better person for it," says John. "After you've been through a life and death situation, your perspective is different. Little things don't bother you so much anymore."

To the rest of us, John's derring-do is astonishing, enviable, bracing. And you don't have to be a muscle flexer, or even a sailor, to be emboldened by the daring adventure. A suburban Errol Flynn. Or at least our own Bill Buckley. As Levinson observes, "The capacity to experience, endure and fight against stagnation is an intrinsic aspect of the struggle toward generativity in middle adulthood."

Not all mid-life risk taking is as swashbuckling as John's twenty-six days before the mast, but that doesn't diminish the challenge. Like John, Janet's perspectives were changed by a life and death situation: the death of her husband. Janet is at the far end of the middle-age spectrum, an attractive woman who might be called a "traditional homemaker." Grown children, no career. Of all the ways she felt herself vulnerable in widowhood, of all the risks she had to take in her newly single status, the most difficult was sexual. Janet grew up with traditional sexual constraints and clear-cut definitions of what nice girls did and didn't do, both before and after marriage. The idea of sleeping with a "date" was unsettling to her, almost promiscuous. The concept of multilovers didn't even occur to her. As a matter of fact, "lovers" in this context is not even in her vocabulary.

Several months after her husband died, she confided to a neighbor, "I'm seeing a really nice man, but I find it hard to be intimate with another man after so many years with my husband."

"You'll feel better about it soon," promised the neighbor.

"I hope so," answered the widow. "You'll be able to tell how I'm doing if you see his gray Oldsmobile in my driveway in the morning."

So every morning the neighbor jumped out of bed to check the driveway, and after several months, she saw the car in front of the garage. "Hooray! Janet finally made it!" she reported to her husband. What's more, when the Oldsmobile pulled out of the driveway, there, affixed to the garage door for all the world to see, was a big red paper heart.

Shortly after, the neighbor ran into Janet in the street.

"I just got married," Janet announced.

"How nice!" said the neighbor. "We did notice that the gray Oldsmobile was staying overnight."

"Oh, no," said Janet. "I married someone else. The gray Oldsmobile was just practice."

Emotional risk taking does not always have a happy ending in the conventional sense. Not until you come to understand that the goal is taking the chance, not the success of the venture. As our high school principal noted, when you take Risk Taking, you can't be sure you'll pass.

My friend Meg is divorced, and with diligence has worked at finding a career and building a life. After testing out the paralegal waters and the retailing life, she found exhilaration in the rather narrow confines of a shopping mall consultant. She turned in her suburban home for an efficiency apartment and, with a certain amount of pride, settled into a life that didn't depend on her children or on a man. All this in the blazing Los Angeles sun, not known to be particularly hospitable to middle-aged females.

Along came Ted, who promised, if not mid-life passion, at least companionship, the one ingredient missing in Meg's well-ordered life. The problem was that Ted lived in St. Louis. After careful thought, Meg waived the blue Pacific, notified her boss and her landlord she was checking out, and followed Ted to St. Louis for what she expected to be two months of a trial friendship. Meg found herself living in the suburban home of Ted's former life, doing the marketing, planting annuals, and cooking for his Saturday night suburban crowd. The two months stretched to six before Meg realized she had bought companionship at the price of autonomy; that she was, in fact, leading the life she had given up in Los Angeles. Meg came home—or went back, depending on your point of view —to L.A.

"Aren't you sorry you gave up your terrific apartment and your great job?" a friend asked Meg.

"Absolutely not," said Meg. "So it didn't work out. If I'd never have done it, I'd have wondered all my life what I had missed."

Meg's complete lack of regret took me by surprise. I had cheered her courage in giving up a hard-won life of independence and security and I was saddened when her gamble failed. What I hadn't grasped was the value of the challenge itself, the compelling need to be absolutely sure one is making optimal use of the remaining time. "We need uncertainty," is the way Gould puts it. "[T]he way of life we shaped in our twenties is under attack. Our certainty that it is the right life for us diminishes . . . now at mid-life we don't need [the certainty]."

If you've ever revealed yourself in new ways, put yourself on the line for the first time, you know that emotional risk taking is the headiest gamble of all. Not until I had lost forty pounds was I able to confront the humiliation—then confess in print—that I customarily allowed an eight-year-old son to take the rap for the cookies I continually ate. The fact that this confession reached a limited audience (the friends who read my book plus everyone my mother stopped on the street) in no way diminished the feeling that by going public with this private mortification I had taken a huge but exhilarating personal risk.

While I felt this admission was monumental—oh, the shame of it!—it was small potatoes compared to the risk taking I was noticing all around me. The most stunning mid-life adventurers were putting everything on the line: ego, pride, economic security. A fifty-five-year-old account executive who left an advertising company to start a small business around his passion for antique American instruments. A computer programmer who flew the corporate coop to open a country inn in Rhode Island. A forty-seven-year-old English teacher, willing to risk that most secure of worlds, a tenured position, for the most insecure, acting. When people ask him if it isn't too late to start an acting career, he answers, "It's too late not to be doing it."

Some of the most interesting men we know are those who are shucking off their original careers, who are depressed—or at least unimpressed—by their putative success. They are reaching deep within themselves for hidden strengths to begin again; to renew themselves. Urgently, they want to, need to, replace the fantasy as soon as it becomes reality, or as soon as they see it will never become a reality.

It's a complicated issue, mid-life men and their work. Many significant strands converge at one vulnerable juncture: the meaning of a man's work and its internal and external satisfactions; how well he's measured up to his early expectations; how well he's met the expectations of others; and always mortality, the ever-present sense of time running out that fuels the important questions: How to make the most of remaining time? How to make the most of one's life? Small wonder that students of human development plumb this rich lode.

"Men perceive a close relationship between life line and career line," notes Neugarten. "Middle age is the time to take stock. Any disparity noted between career expectations and career achievements—that is, whether one is 'on-time' or 'late' in reaching career goals—adds to the heightened awareness of age."

Age. Back again to that ever-present catalyst that seems to underlie so many of our mid-life decisions. Gould, in fact, draws a fascinating link between mortality and work. "Many men see work success as the route to immunity from death," he writes. "We pursue careers with enthusiasm because we accept the mythology of the work world that a man can become invincible with power, money, and status." In time, of course, it becomes clear that this "immunity pact with work" doesn't ward off any of the plagues that are apt to visit mid-life men: illness, problems with their wives and children, death. The pact loses its protective magic when men acknowledge disappointment in their achievements or, ironically, when they assess their triumphs. "By becoming more successful, we learn what more success can't do," says Gould.

This need to take stock, to assess the meaning of one's work, to determine how to make the most of remaining time, is compelling at this vulnerable mid-life moment, whether or not there are disparities between one's expectations and achievements. "If a man at 40 has failed to realize his most cherished dreams, he must begin to come to terms with the failure and arrive at a new set of choices around which to rebuild his life," states Levinson. "If he has succeeded brilliantly, he must consider the meaning and value of his success. . . . Often, a man who has accomplished his goals comes to feel trapped: his success is meaningless and he is now caught within a stultifying situation."

So it is that, whatever their accomplishments, many mid-lifers are compelled to seek deeper meaning in their lives and in their work. They need to utilize their full capacities, they demand respect for their skills, they require inner satisfactions at least as much as the more visible rewards of status or security or money. Some men move precipitously into boldly different ventures; others make more modest adjustments, perhaps changing companies or teaching what they formerly practiced. Still others change the way they do business, leaving an institution to free-lance, or cutting back on work hours to accommodate broader interests. Some men move quickly into new situations, others, as Levinson notes, "tentatively test a variety of new choices, not only out of confusion or impulsiveness but, equally, out of a need to explore, to see what is possible." Whatever the pace or the pursuit, risk is a basic component. And strength.

You notice, no doubt, that I've been talking about the second lives of men only. Nothing chauvinist about it. Many, if not most, mid-life women are doing new things professionally for the first time; their risk, if any, is in entering the marketplace to begin with. Moreover, because of their late entry they seek out (and sometimes find) jobs that meet the deeper needs of their mid-life selves. Women who at an earlier age might have found jobs in public relations or publishing now start their own agencies and services; others are finding at mid-life the satisfactions of the "helping" professions like social work, teaching, social or municipal agencies. Unlike their male contemporaries, very few mid-life women are so far along in their careers that they are bored by them, or so completely self-supporting that they can risk their economic security—not yet, at least. Whatever risks these mid-life women are taking are physical, emotional, sexual—which demand at least as much strength and daring as men call up for their own life changes.

You'll also notice that my favorite risk takers are firmly in mid-life. In fact, they're more likely to be closer to fifty-five than to forty. Perhaps because they are more susceptible to the insistent press of time, they seem to have the fiercest needs to push back horizons, to experience change, to make new beginnings, to have their acts speak for their vigor and vitality.

For example, let me tell you about a lawyer we know. His story is not dramatic, but it does bespeak a quiet courage in the search for "authenticity" that illuminates the most hopeful mid-life stories. He is a man who takes pride in his profession, and in a community of colleagues. Recently he became dismayed at the human environment of his law firm where he has been a partner for twenty-five years; at the inability of the lawyers to get along with one another; at the squabbling over division of profits. So one day he told his wife, "I want to finish my career with dignity, in a more wholesome atmosphere where colleagues support and respect each other, even when they have differing points of view."

"That's great," said his wife, wanting him to be happy as well as productive.

Several months later he reported, "I've found a wonderful new firm. They want me to start a new department. We're enthusiastic about each other. However, they point out quite properly that the risk is all on my side."

"Risk? What risk?" asked the wife. She hadn't realized there was any hazard in the decision.

"The risk that it won't work out, that I won't be able to deliver what they expect. I'm confident about it, or I wouldn't be making the move. But there is a risk."

"Oh." The wife reported waves of anxiety, a slow churning in the stomach.

"If you feel at all uncomfortable about it, I'll stay where I am. I have security. I have retirement benefits. I can continue where I am."

"No, no," said the wife hastily. "I can't have you spending your days in an office you hate." Why not? Lots of people don't like their work, she thought. What about the tuition bills coming up? The security. We're too old to start over.

"Great!" said the husband appreciatively. "Because this is no way to live."

I really don't have a choice, she thought. We'll make out. We have to make out. I'll get a job. It will be a terrific challenge for me, too. . . .

"You know," continued the husband philosophically, "I knew I had to make the move when I read about a woman who years ago cooperated with the House Un-American Activities Committee over the Hollywood blacklist. She was divorced, and bringing up two kids by herself. She named names—and she never forgave herself for it, for selling out. Even though she was the sole support of her kids.

"That's exactly the way I feel. I don't want to sell out for the economics. I don't want to regret any of my big decisions—the ones I take, and especially the ones I was afraid to take."

It's an admirable, principled stand, and I hope to hell it works out. I am the wife.

10

STAIRWAYS
TO PARADISE

When she is alone at home, my friend Pam occasionally sits down at the upright, pulls out her simplified piano music, and burrows back into some spirited Gershwin and Cole Porter tunes. "I'm playing and singing my heart out," she reports, "with lots of pedal so I sound wonderful.

Pam, you'll note, is not singing the blues. She may be recalling her salad days and feeling, now that her youngest child is setting up an independent domicile, that her time is here, too. I don't want to make too much of this, but there is a moment in the middle years of women, especially married women, when promise is in the air and opportunities seem infinite. "It's all possible," says Pam. "The question is, what do we want?"

True. There is a headlong sense of liberation and opportunity. Anything goes. Neugarten recognized it in the study on human development at the University of Chicago. Of the 2,000 participants, she wrote: "Most of the women interviewed feel that the most conspicuous characteristic of middle age is the sense of increased freedom . . . a period in which latent talents and capacities can be put to use in new directions."

This sometimes comes as a surprise, observes Dr. Robert N. Butler, professor of geriatrics and adult development at Mount Sinai School of Medicine. "It's often writ that come the empty nest and the woman doesn't know what to do," he says, "but studies show that many women feel absolutely ecstatic and liberated, and move into different opportunities and occupations and roles."

Pam, for example, sees that disparate experiences of her life have come together in her job of administering the county office for the disabled—the home economist and health education, the mental health work, the studies in home and family life, the community service, the years with the League of Women Voters, even the magazine writing job before she married. For the first time, in mid-life, she sees how it all fits together and makes sense. Also for the first time, she has confidence that the pieces will hold and she'll survive as a worker, even if the government funding that supports her office runs out, as it threatens to each year.

This mid-life moment of expectation is special to women, a moment their male colleagues are not likely to understand, let alone share. And the reason, of course, is that they are finally free of their primary day-to-day obligations to home and children. Whatever else middle-aged women did during their twenties and thirties and into their forties—and many of them did work—it was all in addition to running the home and raising the kids. The working mother (not father) found a baby-sitter or stayed home with a sick child. The mother was never truly free to go on the road to sell insurance or promote a book, or take a client to dinner—at least not without a lot of arranging and explaining. And permission. For many a woman, it wasn't even easy to get her husband to pick up the dry cleaning on Saturday morning. What's more, we mid-life wives didn't even expect him to. As Anne Morrow Lindbergh said, "What a circus act we women perform every day of our lives."

And then, at some moment in the life of her family, a woman declares her liberation. At some point she understands that she is free of these long-held responsibilities, that she no longer has to dance in three rings simultaneously, that she is responsible only for herself. As Pam says, "You realize you are really peripheral to your children's lives. Then it hits you: Who have you got but yourself?" The double whammy is that many a mid-life wife not only feels peripheral to her husband's life as well but also feels that he is essential to hers. Throw in the sex-blind reminder that usually surfaces at these times—*there's more time behind than ahead*—and you have a powerful energizer. Motive plus opportunity. An actuarial imperative. *If not now, when?* As Gould notes, "Upon the realization of their own mortality, women feel an increased mandate to act on their own behalf."

Shucking off the dependent—and depended-upon—role is a powerful drive of mid-life women, and one that Gould has studied at length. It is closely allied, he believes, to the "protector myth" that women, especially those in their mid-life decade, fear they cannot survive alone. "The greatest inhibiting fear for a woman is caused by the false assumption: 'It is impossible to live without a protector in life.'"

The only way to regain control of their lives and prove the assumption false, Gould believes, is "through definitive action." And definitive, explicit action is exactly what I've noticed a good many mid-life women are taking. Rosalie now goes on annual week-long camping trips with a group of strangers; her protector of thirty-three years stays home tinkering with his car and his hi-fi set. Marilyn stepped from a volunteer job at a social agency into the fast-track urban real estate lane, and with the proceeds from several intoxicating condominium sales took her protector of three decades and his mother to Europe. "It was terrific to pay for the trip," she says, exuberantly acknowledging that the purse strings confer power (as our protectors have always known). Nell, after many years of full-time community activity, started law school at forty-eight; she tries to save weekends to sail with her protector, but occasionally has to forego crewing when an exam looms.

All this newly declared independence is heady for mid-life women. It fosters an unaccustomed sense of self and, for many, an unfamiliar joy in pleasing oneself. This, Pam reminds me, is often a new experience for the nurturers of others who always did what was expected of them, who never felt altogether entitled to a separate identity. Pam, who has nurtured, guided, cajoled, berated, and enjoyed three now-grown children and a husband, put it this way: "Pleasing one's middle-aged self doesn't come easy. It's hard to listen to your own needs, since we are so used to pleasing others."

Pam is struggling to loosen the grip of what psychologist David Gutmann calls "the parental imperative." By this he means a culturally imposed requirement that mothers must nurture and fathers be powerful, all "in the service of family and ultimately species survival." When children are grown and traditional sex roles no longer required for the survival of society, parents are not only free to explore their own needs but are also tempted to expand those traditional sex roles. Indeed, says Gutmann, "There appears to be a comprehensive developmental event of middle and later life, involving strongly bonded mates, that acts to reverse or at least equalize the domestic status of the partners, and that tends to redistribute the so-called masculine and feminine traits among them."

Small wonder that when mid-life women come into their own, they often challenge, even defy, long-established relationships. Men, you'll remember, are usually doing their marital business under an entirely different long-term contract. When women confront and question the long-held ways of doing business, they threaten the relationship, rock the equilibrium, upset the homeostasis. "Most women in this society are not able to break through the protector myth without in some measure blaming their husbands," says Gould. This only hints at the subterranean resentment and bitterness that hang over the dining room table, spoken or unspoken, when women feel they are wasting their talents and energies. "They are ready to challenge the myth that men don't love women who have their own power," says Gould.

Well, some men do and some don't. And those who do, don't all the time. Mark loved his trip to Europe courtesy of Marilyn, but still expects his bed made every morning. Arthur is proud of Nell at law school, occasionally miffed if she can't sail with him, and always annoyed if she has to study when he has to entertain a customer. As Gould notes, "Husbands love less when change costs them something; they love more when change benefits them."

Moreover, a man's grip on his own mid-life passage often dictates the way he will accept changes in the shape of his marriage. "A man who feels that his own youthfulness is in jeopardy may be more threatened than pleased by his wife's invitation to modify their lives," notes Levinson. "In some families, the wife's growing assertiveness and freedom are accompanied by the husband's severe decline." It is almost as if there is a finite wellspring of vitality to a marriage, and when the wife draws more than her accustomed share, less is available for the husband.

A woman's move toward independence and autonomy can spring from factors other than her intimations of mortality. One prime cause is the end of her marriage. Here there is no longer the need to confront the protector myth; there is no longer a protector. It's sink or swim. And whether the marriage has ended due to death or divorce or desertion, most women are buoyant and, sooner or later, they swim.

Jennifer is a woman I know who woke up one day, literally, demeaned and deserted. She promptly lost twenty pounds to get herself to lean fighting weight, took a short-term accounting course, and got a job in a high-powered firm. Two years later she's still at the firm and contemplating business school.

"My life is dividing into neat segments," she said to me. "For twenty-one years I was my parents' child. I lived at home. For the next twenty-one years I was my husband's wife. I entertained his customers, ran his errands, raised three sons. Now I have a third life —my own." Jennifer has taken charge of her life with breathtaking dispatch. When she wants to see a play, she buys two tickets and invites a male friend to join her. When she wants to ski, she packs up and goes by herself. When she wants to see friends, she cooks dinner and invites us all over. At the rate she's going, she has time for two more lives—both her own.

You'll notice that as women take over responsibility for their lives, they also take on some of the characteristics that are traditionally associated with the protector persona. When Levinson discusses the time-honored family roles, he notes, "The qualities regarded as masculine involve success in work, getting ahead, earning one's fortune for the sake of self and family . . . feminine [qualities] involve building the nest and ministering to the multiple needs of husband and children." Precisely the role switch that Jennifer has just perfected.

What's more, the swap is likely to serve her well as she moves into her third and fourth lives, according to a study by the National Policy Center on Women and Aging. "The women who had the best adjustment to aging could be categorized as androgynous rather than stereotypically feminine, becoming more assertive or more male oriented across a lifespan," says Dr. Marilyn R. Block, its director. "It may be that the stereotypical attributes of male and female just don't work after middle age, and people who can cast those off and adjust to a new style of behavior do well. We can't explain why it happens; we've just observed it."

Redefining traditional roles in the mid-life years is a continuing concern of adult development theorists. Levinson writes of the need for men to integrate what he calls the "Masculine/Feminine polarity." In Gould's study, which encompassed both men and women, he observed, "Both of us are driven to rework our concept of the male and female aspects of ourselves . . . as men we're striving for release from our stereotyped masculinity and opening ourselves up to need, uncertainty, anxiety, and ambiguity. As women we're striving for release from our stereotyped femininity and taking on new strengths, autonomy, freedom, novelty and self-confidence." However, as Gail Sheehy shrewdly observed, all this is from a male perspective: "All the male researchers into adult development agree . . . that the path to replenishment in mid-life is through nurturing, teaching, and serving others."

That may be what middle-aged men ought to do; it isn't necessarily what they *are* doing. While working women of middle age (or of any age) are likely to become more independent, competitive, assertive—all traditionally male characteristics—most of their male colleagues don't seem to be rushing into nurturing, teaching, or serving others—all traditionally female venues. Very few men give up their power perches in corporate, institutional, or professional America solely to replenish themselves through these pursuits. When men do teach or take on far-reaching community service commitments, it usually burnishes the image of their primary work at least as much as it replenishes the new teacher or community activist. It's good business for the law firm when a partner teaches at a law school; it enhances the public image of a corporation when an officer heads the United Fund drive.

It is easier, it seems, for women to give up "feminine" qualities than for men to relinquish what is regarded as "masculine." Perhaps because women are more successful at this mid-life transformation, they are, during these years, particularly lively and interesting (more interesting than mid-life men, according to most women and not a few men). Not only are many of them seeking new worlds, but they are also more thoughtful about the quest, more knowing in the pursuit, and they are proceeding with wisdom and humor. You can't beat that for good company.

What middle-aged women have going for them is that they know themselves better than young women (and young men) in the same pursuit. They know their strengths and weaknesses. They are sure of the talents they can call on for certain tasks. And they have that high-octane fuel of wanting to—needing to—establish their own identity.

What middle-aged women have going against them, of course, is middle age. They quickly discover that by conventional standards they are virtually unemployable, at least on the level they regard themselves as competent. Ask any mid-life woman who tries to get a job commensurate with her abilities. It is not that she has an inflated view of her talents—many employers acknowledge that these middle-aged applicants can do the work—it's just that the company doesn't hire from the outside at that level. That it already has a large enough pool of talent to fish in. That she is overqualified for the job. That. That. That. Mainly that she is perceived as too old.

There are some women who become dispirited by society's perception of them. They walk into job interviews apologizing that their skills are rusty, explaining that they have spent the last twenty years raising children, giving prospective employers every reason not to hire them. But happily, more and more of them are refusing to accept that verdict, refusing to adopt that stance, refusing, as Laurie described it, to join the attack on themselves. Perhaps they are emboldened by the women's movement or encouraged by their daughters, but more and more women these days are determined to prevail. They might have overheard Laurie state her credo: "If they say you're too old, you say, 'Bullshit, I'm not!'"

If employment is an immediate economic necessity—and God knows, for more and more of us that is the case—we take what work we can get. But if we have the luxury of a little time, our capacity for self-employment can be breathtaking. Laurie may be unduly optimistic when she says, "I firmly believe that any woman with a little creativity, some brains, and a lot of energy can find work. Plus, 'a little bit of bloomin' luck!' as Alfred P. Doolittle said."

Aside from the women who in mid-life get specific training—in social work, law, urban planning, computer programming—or those who have the funds to back themselves in a business venture, there are still women of energy and ingenuity who parlay their strengths into rewarding work. It's no surprise that Laurie is one of them.

Through her years of paid and volunteer employment, Laurie

has accumulated a variety of skills. In her last job she was a museum "development officer," an all-purpose job description that covered grant proposals, budget making and membership drives, in addition to public relations, fund-raising campaigns, and special events. When that job ended—not, I hasten to explain, because of age—Laurie assessed her strengths: a talent for people, a wealth of ideas on practically anything, a love of words and graphics, and an enthusiasm for work. What Laurie carved out for herself was a free-lance consultancy on practically anything. She ghosts articles, writes speeches, dreams up promotions, designs brochures, writes newsletters—all the promotion, publicity, editorial, advertising, and creative planning that small businesses often need and despair of finding.

Where Laurie has, and likes, a one-person shop, my friend Kim has a whole PR agency (actually half—she has a partner). She started as a free lance, now has sixteen employees. In her charming Southern manner she hustles business and competes for clients—successfully, I might add—just as if she were a young hotshot male. Her only nod to being a middle-aged female is when she bemoans not having a mentor. So when she hears about some wise and experienced man of letters or of business or of the law, she disarmingly explains to him her quest for guidance and advice.

Jean never had a mentor either (middle-aged women often have men but rarely mentors); she followed the networking route instead. Networking is a term currently in vogue for an association of colleagues that share some key experience. Originally, as we all know, that key experience was schooling at an elite university and/or employment in an Establishment institution, and the colleagues were always male. Now women have borrowed that support system. In Jean's network, there is no education requirement (some women, including Jean, didn't complete their higher education until they were in their forties) and there is no employment; the key experience is that mid-life drive to find rewarding work. What Jean did was open an office to counsel this network on résumé writing, job interviewing, assessing options, and related concerns. Then she wrote a how-to book for those who couldn't get to her office. Because Jean is a savvy businesswoman, she also took on some business clients for whom she head-hunts. These pay the rent and en-able her to do what she is passionately committed to: helping her mid-life networkers build their stairways to paradise.

A lot of women manage very well alone, thank you, building on familiar strengths. A woman I know in Pennsylvania, whose down-home cooking was lavishly praised, opened a now-flourishing, home-style farm restaurant, then a country inn, wrote two cookbooks, and has just taped a cooking show for national distribution on television. Other women parlay the skills they honed as volunteers: corresponding secretaries who set up word-processing facilities; newsletter editors who offer free-lance editorial services; a former researcher who set up an electronic information retrieval service; a PTA president whose expertise in education issues was welcomed by a prestigious education foundation.

Some women who don't have easily transferable skills are particularly perceptive about their strengths. My friend Stella is one of these. Quite by accident, through a volunteer project for a social service agency, she found a field that admirably suits her talents: oral history. On her first visit to the agency's oral history collection, she realized, "I really want to do this. I can do this." She promptly and thoughtfully planned the steps to a profession; first she volunteered in a clerical capacity, then learned how to interview, attended a professional conference where, she remembers, "I found a world of oral historians that I loved," and finally took a university course for professional training and credentials. She exemplifies Gould's belief that "commitment is what discriminates mid-life activity from the activities of the preceding years." Now Stella runs an oral history service whose clients are universities, corporations, and individuals who want to preserve the historical recollections of their associates.

What makes Stella's new mid-life career so intriguing is that it is uniquely suited to middle age. It calls on special qualities that younger people usually haven't had time to develop, and it satisfies yearnings that younger people simply don't have. "The skills you develop in any leadership role in the community over the years are useful for oral history, for encouraging people to share their personal stories," Stella explains. "One of the most useful is listening to people. Another is learning to respond to them so they will think well of the need to serve the community as well as their own needs."

There are also, Stella reminds me, the special satisfactions of an oral historian that are best appreciated in mid-life: the freedom from having to be scintillating and interesting oneself when there is someone interesting to listen to, and, for anyone who has had a good college experience, a nostalgia for research. Finally, Stella put her finger on what is probably the most appealing aspect of this work, at least for those of us in mid-life: "The sense of being connected to something beyond yourself," she said. "In your forties, it's nice to have a connection with something that will last."

Even if other types of mid-life work do not have that hint of immortality, they usually provide the primary qualities that women seek when they start to shape their own lives at mid-life—realistic gratification and recognition. Mastery over their own lives. Self-determination. A sense of identity. My friend Marie, who heads public relations for a large psychiatric hospital, says, "The esteem I get in my job is really important to me."

When work does bring gratification and recognition, for many women it may also provide a special kind of victory over earlier insecurities and fears that perhaps prevented, or delayed, breaking out sooner. For myself, for instance, it had to do with barricading myself in my home office behind typewriter and telephone, not to mention those forty extra pounds of insulating fat. By the time I was able to shed that weight—my own middle-aged mandate—I was also able to write the intimate story of that journey from fat to thin. And my publishers, not content that my fat lady confessions of conduct unbecoming an adult remain between hard covers, wanted me to broadcast my shame, tell the whole world that I filed the Raisinets under *R* in my desk drawer. They were handing me a big-time challenge. I was petrified.

Let me explain. Other people can handle public appearances with poise, self-possession, presence of mind. Not me. Even Jack Horner could stick in his thumb and pull out aplomb. The prospect of speaking in (much less to) groups larger than six terrifies me. When I went to my first PTA meeting and the program chairman asked each of us to introduce ourselves, I couldn't get the two words out. So here is Judy of Publicity talking about department store appearances, call-in radio shows, media markets. And television. *Television?* As Russell Baker wrote about his own book tour, "The idea of going on television and making all America fall in love with you doesn't leave much mental space for clear thinking."

"Don't worry," says Judy, picking me off the floor. "We'll start you off easy to give you some practice."

For some friendly coaching I call on my pal Laurie. Laurie knows about a lot of things, and what she doesn't know, she improvises. She'll walk through an archeological exhibit, look at a few shards of pottery and a tool or two, and reconstruct the conversation of two Cro-Magnon housewives.

"Hey," says one. "Max brought home this hunk of buffalo last night. Again buffalo. The kids are sick and tired of buffalo every night. Whaddaya having for dinner?"

"Sadie, you wouldn't believe! Have I got a recipe for you . . ."

So Laurie primes me for the big time. And the reason I'm willing to risk making a middle-aged fool of myself is that I do feel, on the one hand, a new surge of mid-life confidence and, on the other, an equally novel inclination toward daredevil, if-not-now-when undertakings.

Judy's idea of practice is a press interview with a metropolitan daily. The reporter and I are to meet at the Plaza Hotel; we can go to the Palm Court, suggests Judy. I like that. When I was a teenager in New York, my friends and I would go to the Palm Court for a glamorous adventure. We would eat extravagant pastries and sit for hours at a little marble table. While a string group played quietly we pretended we were exotic princesses, or at least debutantes. I thought an hour in the Palm Court was the height of sophistication. It was somewhat like wearing your mother's high heel shoes in public; you only hope no one notices that you don't really fit in.

As soon as I meet the reporter, she leads me out toward Fifth Avenue and Central Park. It's a perfect day. Crisp clear air, dappled sunlight. We wander through the park, chatting about our children, our husbands, our work.

"This will be fine," says the reporter, spotting an empty bench in the zoo and taking out her tape recorder. As I watch the elephant spraying water with his trunk, I think, Whatever made me think I was ready for the Palm Court?

Then one day the phone rings. It's Judy. "Are you sitting down? The 'Today' show called."

Well, after a couple of months on the hustings, I know that a telephone call is not a definite commitment. I've learned why appearances are only penciled in. And I have a friend who knows exactly how the "Today" show works.

"They shave at the show," says my "Today" informant.

"Of course they do," I answer. "Except for Gene Shalit, they're a pretty clean-cut bunch."

"No, no. If the interview doesn't get going in the first few seconds, they shave it, cut it down. All of a sudden there'll be a commercial."

I'm still in my bravura mode, so I think, What could be so hard about looking into the camera—see, the one with the red light on top—and waving, "Hey, Ma. Look at me!"

"Aren't you nervous?" a friend asks.

The answer is yes and no.

For example, I haven't exactly slept since Judy first called.

For example, the amplified beat that follows me around is not an ear-bending disco rhythm but my very own heart.

And what would you say to a blazing headache every time a friendly person says, "Good morning. How are you TODAY?"

That's the yes answer.

The no answer has to do with the general perspective. As Rick wrote from Africa, "The whole idea is so boggling and awesome that it is almost too much to get nervous about. Our worry quotas don't include things like 'Today' show appearances."

He's absolutely right. We are observers of the "Today" show, not participants. Crossing the line—that tangle of cables—and actually entering the set is almost incomprehensible. A "Today" show appearance has nothing whatsoever to do with my life.

So at 6:30 A.M. on the morning of the show, a limo drives me to the studio. Rafe is with me. He is there for moral and, if necessary, physical support. I frantically study my book as if heading into a final exam. What was that book about anyway?

Rafe tries to put me at ease. "Would you like to see a show this weekend?"

"Shut up!"

As I'm trying to concentrate, a local news bulletin breaks into the soothing radio music. "Con Ed reports a power failure in parts of the metropolitan area . . ."

I should have known. I had always expected to be wiped out. I just hadn't gotten the details right. All along I was waiting to be preempted by a national event of great importance. Or get sick. Or, more likely, wake up with paralysis of the vocal cords. But I never figured on a power failure. What irony! The show would go on . . . but no one could see it.

There are several things I can report about the experience. The Green Room is beige. The coffee is strong. Tom Brokaw eats bagels. And there is a guest sheet to sign. Future guests can flip through while awaiting their appearances and see who inhabited the Green Room before them. Like the guest books at country inns. "Ooh, look! Winston Churchill was here in 1937."

About the interview I'm not too clear on exactly what happened. I think everything went fine.

I sail out of Rockefeller Center. I've made it. The Big Time. Rick, on first hearing of the adventure, foretold the sequence of coming events. "Mother, *the 'Today' show!!!* That means best-seller, movie rights, Hers column, house on Nantucket, winters in Gstaad, photos in *WWD,* a regular table at Four Seasons." Meanwhile, it's only 8:45 A.M., and I have three and a half hours until a lunch appointment. While these coming attractions germinate, I can cruise up and down Fifth Avenue, giving the hometown folks a chance to ask for autographs.

"Hey," they'll say. "Aren't you . . . didn't I just see you . . . Wow!"

"Excuse me." A woman stops me in front of St. Patrick's Cathedral.

"Yes?" I flash her a brilliant smile.

"Which way is Madison Avenue?"

11

CAUGHT IN
THE MIDDLE

"My mother broke her hip," says my friend Maggie. "She's feeling better now, but I guess it's a taste of things to come." Maggie's voice is flat with conflicting emotions: relief that things aren't worse and dread that they probably soon will be.

Most of the middle-aged people I know are like Maggie, caught between the children who no longer need us and the parents who are about to. We feel both connected to and separate from the generations that bracket us. In this continuum we are preoccupied, as Neugarten observed, with "how one should relate to both younger and older persons and how to act one's age."

It isn't easy. Most of us aren't yet certain just how old we really are. Moreover, one constant of our middle years is a muddle of relationships, what Margaret Drabble in *The Middle Ground* calls "a thick clutter of cross-references." We are caught in the middle, sandwiched between our children and our parents, between our past and our future and, as Drabble writes, "free of neither: the past stretches back too densely, it is too thickly populated, the future has not yet thinned out." In this middle ground of ironic juxtapositions, we are at once adults with often childish diversions and children with adult aspirations. We tend to be adult heavies with our children and struggling children with our parents. Our relationship with both generations is animated by intimations of mortality. On the one hand we yearn to leave the best of ourselves—our human legacy —with (perhaps in) our children; on the other, we are forced to confront our mortality through our parents. Our parents are our advance guard, running interference for us, the buffer that shields us. They are all that stands between us and . . . whatever follows. When they go, we're next. That's heavy baggage for a relationship to carry. It invites complex and puzzling feelings and unwitting misunderstandings.

Perhaps this is why we spend so much of our time discussing our families. If it's not our children, it's our parents. Especially it's our parents. Sometimes they are the topic sentence, the subject, of our concern; sometimes they are peripheral, a conditional clause, but they are always—well, almost always—an essential element in the conversation. We don't need Neugarten to remind us that "concern over an aging parent or parent-in-law has come to be part of the psychological baggage that most adults carry around in their heads." We do, however, have a wide range of emotions as we cover this main topic: concern, dread, pride, despair, anxiety, joy, exasperation, compassion, impatience, and guilt. Always guilt. We didn't call this week. (Gulp.) We aren't doing enough. (Oh, God.) It's time for our expected visit. (Again!) Even when we feel our most loving, there is always a nagging underlay: Why don't we feel this way all the time? When I call my mother—the least demanding of parents—she often ends our conversations with what I am prepared to accept as perfectly innocent questions: Are you coming to town this week? Will we see you soon? What are you doing? Straightforward queries asked, I'm willing to believe, only in fond interest. Yet each time I hang up the phone, a long-ago skit by Mike Nichols and Elaine May flashes to mind.

Son (after just such a long-distance remark): Mom, you make me feel so guilty.

Mother: If I could only believe that.

Guilt—justified or not—seems to animate much of our dealings with our parents. And the worst, most guilt-provoking part, of course, is that our concern and anxiety are, ultimately, not for our parents at all but for ourselves. Even our short-term apprehensions are for ourselves. We no longer see our parents as independent (if they are) and autonomous, but primarily in their relationship to us. What do their leisure, their activities, their health, the whole conduct of their lives mean to us? How does all this affect us? Florence Shelley, co-author of *When Your Parents Grow Old*, diagnoses the anxiety and guilt. "It's fear of the burden about to be imposed, emotionally and psychically," she says. "Fear that we will lose control of our own lives."

Perhaps that's why we are reluctant to make our check-in phone calls. The telephone becomes our instrument of torture; we'll shun the messenger before it delivers the unwanted message. Of course, the messages we most dread don't wait for our calls; they come to us. Those we make are most likely to stir up the old familiar guilt: We haven't been around lately, we haven't been paying enough attention, the neighbor's grandchildren have come for a visit . . . okay, okay, we get the message.

The last time Laurie got the message was when her mother-in-law came up from Florida for a visit. Laurie is my pal who can dream up an answer for practically anything, even guilt, so she gave a lunch for her mother-in-law. She invited several of her friends and their mothers; the ticket of admission was an older-generation female. None of the mothers knew each other, and what do you think they talked about? Their grandchildren? Their daughters who don't call often enough? Their sons, who may or may not be worthy of these women? What they spent two and a half hours discussing was the relative merits of Leslie Howard versus Ronald Colman. I felt terrible that my mother missed lunch. She would have made a strong case for Charles Boyer.

Most of the time we children aren't treated to the romantic fantasies of our aging parents, at least not that we know of. Perhaps it was the memory of Charles Boyer that prompted the despair of a recent conversation.

"Everything's falling apart," Mother begins.

"What's the matter?" I hear the anxiety in my voice. I wish it showed more compassion.

"It's my hair. It's been falling out."

"Everyone's hair falls out sometimes. Have you seen a doctor?"

"Yes. He says it's from tension and stress." Hmmm. I consider the main sources. There's my father . . . and me. "He gave me some stuff to rub in my hair. He says it's coming along just fine," she continues, gloomily.

"Well," I say, relief flooding me. "Of all the things that could go wrong, that doesn't seem too serious."

"And that's not all," continues Mother. "My bridge broke."

The parts of the machine are breaking down. Hair and teeth so far. Not bad, I think, after eighty years. But to Mother they are the packaging, her visible front to the world. More than most people, my mother, the octogenarian who feels younger than fifty when she doesn't have a cold, believes there are only three ages of man: youth, middle age, and "You're looking great." At this moment of her life appearances are reality. What's more, these erosions of her health are only the beginning, she fears. That prospect terrifies her. And me.

Back to guilt. And anger. A tangle of emotions at seeing our parents fail and not being able to do anything about it. "There is such heartbreak in seeing someone you love become ineffective," says psychiatric social worker Carol Froehlich softly, talking about her mother who had recently died. "You carry a mental picture of your mother at her peak. It's hard to make peace with that unresponsive woman who bears no resemblance to what she was." Some people are never able to make peace with the fact of a failing parent. I know more than one man with a mother in a nursing home who begs his wife, "Why don't you go visit her? It doesn't hurt you as much as it hurts me." Dr. Stephen DeBerry, a psychologist and specialist in geriatrics, explains, "The basis of our guilt is our impotence in the face of aging and death. In their mortality one cannot help but read one's own epitaph." Here we are, reminded yet again, and in the most poignant way, of our own advancing mortality.

Moreover, it's at this vulnerable moment that we are apt to fall heir to that most dreaded role: caretaker. Inevitably, as our parents age and falter, they really do need more care and attention. And just as inevitably, that burden falls on their daughters. This is not to say that sons don't have the same sense of obligation and commitment as daughters. "We are accustomed to thinking of the woman as the kin-keeper in the family network," states Neugarten, "but it is men as well as women who worry about their parents and who report that a change in the parent has produced a change in their own lives."

True. Sons may have equal concern, but it is the daughters who are on call. "It is absolutely universal in the United States that the women of the family carry the major responsibility for older parents," says Dr. Rose Dobrof, professor of Social Work, Hunter College, and director of the Brookdale Center on Aging, who has observed thousands of aging parents and their middle-aged children. "When we find a son as primary care giver, he is always in that position by default."

As Maggie flew to her mother's hospital bed, she remembers, "I went feeling anxious about my mother. I fussed over her and she loved it, although she kept saying I shouldn't. But I have a good relationship with both my parents, so I didn't have anything to settle with them. And as it happened, I had a wonderful time with my father. We had a degree of closeness we hadn't had in years."

For others similar circumstances can send up a dust storm of complicated emotions. Lorna, another woman I know, got the same precipitous, chilling phone call: Mother broke hip . . . in hospital . . . come at once. "I couldn't have gotten through that reverse dependency of my mother's without my friends," she recalls. "I was wiped out, overburdened. With all the medical complications, it was difficult to lead my own life for a year. I had a lot of resentment. At one point I considered getting psychiatric help." Lorna paused. "I envy a friend of mine whose sick mother is three thousand miles away."

The very act of caring for our ill parents, DeBerry explains, often stirs up dormant feelings of love, of anger, of resentment—"vestiges of unfinished business within the family. In situations where old feelings and conflicts are reactivated, there is inevitably going to be guilt." What often happens is that we throw ourselves into this new caretaking role with a vengeance. We aren't exactly sure just how much a frail mother can do for herself or how much company a widowed father really wants, so we do everything. We hover, we boss, we make decisions for them. We call daily, visit frequently. It all makes us feel so much better. Our overzealousness either betrays our guilt or, for many, becomes an insurance policy, taken out so we won't feel guilty. Either way, we are prompted by what writer Judith Wax called our "guilt-edged insecurities."

Wilma is a woman who by circumstance (and perhaps temperament) has made caretaking her calling. Her father is frail and nearly blind; he lives with a devoted housekeeper. For two years after her mother died, Wilma drove fifty miles to visit him every day. Then she cut back to three or four times a week. She used to be a substitute teacher, but that is no longer possible. The first time she wanted to take a vacation, her father had an anxiety attack that kept him in bed for two weeks. "Now I can get away for a little while, but I have to be near a telephone," says Wilma. "At least I don't feel guilty. I know I'm doing absolutely everything I can. I feel badly to see someone I love getting senile, but, no, I don't feel guilty in any way."

Wilma's burden may sound extreme but it is little heavier than many other middle-aged children's. Many look in on their parents daily, some take a parent in to live with them, others support them in nursing homes, adding a financial burden to the emotional one. The extent and type of involvement may differ, but these middle-aged caretakers are likely to share common feelings. Here is the scenario that DeBerry rolls out: "Resentment over time lost in one's own life, guilt feelings over the resentment, irritation over feeling guilty, and physical illness from holding the irritation inside." Wilma, for instance, never actually complains that she has essentially lost control of her life, but I just realized that her frequent and debilitating back spasms may not be entirely organic.

Ironically, Wilma may not realize that her father is probably also suffering from similar guilt. There is more than enough of it, it seems, to go around. "Guilt is a two-sided family phenomenon," DeBerry explains. "It is experienced by both the adult and the child." The parent, no less than the child, feels guilty about being dependent, needing care. How many times have we heard old people say to their middle-aged children: "The worst thing is to have to come to you. . . . No house is big enough for two families. . . . The day I can't take care of myself is the day I'll take all my pills." That the threat of suicide has no correlation with its incidence betrays the anguish our parents suffer and don't express overtly. "Feelings of being a burden, of losing one's self-respect, of being a nuisance, are very real and very common " says De-Berry. In other cultures where age is revered and the oldest is the wisest, such despair over being dependent in one's old age is not common.

Given the value our own culture places on independence, it is probably not surprising that both aging parent and middle-aged child so often feel the same overwhelming sense of mutual guilt over the concern, love, and need each has for the other. Moreover, when neither parent nor child is candid with the other about these fears and resentments, feelings of self-recrimination and blame multiply on both sides. It may help all of us to believe DeBerry's assertion that "guilt is unavoidable. It is a condition of human existence." It will surely help to follow his advice: "Remember, guilt is on both sides of the generations. It can be talked about, acknowledged, partially resolved and most important of all, given meaning." (A rather different meaning emerges if we consider that guilt, in our culture a seemingly inevitable legacy passed on without regard to genetic heritage, also informs our dealing with our children. But when we are the parents, we are apt to have an ambivalent attitude toward it. As a friend of mine says, "Guilt? Don't knock it. It's the only weapon we have.")

The impotent child caretaker is just one in the welter of paradoxes that engulf the middle-aged and our parents. There is also the continuing irony that we don't have a firm grip on our own status: Are we child or grown-up? Neither? Both? The questions are especially perplexing now that our parents are often living into their eighties and nineties. Moreover, as we try to understand our position on this lengthening continuum, we find that the answers are without precedent. "We have very few guides to how a middle-aged child behaves toward an eighty-five-year-old mother when he is a child and a spouse and a parent and a grandparent," says Dobrof. "We need a new etiquette."

No wonder the generational affiliations blur. "At this time there is also a sense of becoming one's own parents," says Rosenbaum. "Seeing ourselves as our mothers and fathers were at our age. Remembering how they were at this time." And at some point a quasi-role reversal seems to take place as the child becomes father of the father. Not just the obvious catapulting into "parental" responsibilities when a parent is ill or incapacitated, but a slowly shifting relationship that is acknowledged, perhaps even unconsciously, by both parties. For instance, the first time I noticed a tilt to our family configuration was when Rafe and I had dinner with his parents, and his father, heretofor the check grabber, didn't say a word as Rafe paid the bill, and we all understood that paternal role had passed to our generation. It was a small but chilling rite of passage. "In one way or another, we are losing the last vestiges of our parents' protection," explains Gould. "Even if both parents are alive, vigorous and independent, a role reversal takes place, and gradually we are standing in their place."

Paradoxically, it's a swap we aren't entirely pleased to make. Despite our lifelong struggle for independence and autonomy, we still nurture a child within who is loath to sail out of our parents' safe harbor. Standing in their place is a constant reminder of our mortality. Moreover, we still need their approval and love, still yearn to be cared for. Because poignant incongruity is a condition natural to the middle-aged child, I understood completely when a fifty-nine-year-old nurse I know confessed her longing to be mothered still by her own eighty-five-year-old incapacitated parent, and her sadness that she—a professional trained to nurture—now has the mothering role. "It's very hard to break out of the child state," she said, "especially when you need comforting yourself."

If we feel ambivalent about the generational role reversal, consider how our parents feel. They hate it. They resist giving up their place to us in multifarious ways. They may have had to retire from their jobs, relinquish their places of leadership in the community, step out of the center of activity, but they still have us to advise, direct, correct, and guide. And a lot more time in which to do it. "Our parents hang on to whatever power they have over us to fortify their sense of safety," says Gould. And because we have the illusion our parents can still keep us safe, we allow them, he adds, "a small, but often irritating, degree of power over us." Here is the recognizable experience of an editor I know who had just lost his job. When Tom went to talk with his father, the seventy-nine-year-old moved right into his old protector role, discussing ways of getting the fifty-year-old son a job. "It was just like his arranging for my first job thirty years ago," says Tom. "My parents never seem to get past seeing me as their dependent child. They still call Alice and me 'the children.' I hate it. We are not the children. We have children of our own."

Shucking off our filial personae is a struggle we middle-aged children are not likely to master, certainly not easily. The odds are against us. There are, first of all, our own small pockets of resistance to becoming entirely grown up. And there are our parents—living and/or dead. For example, I am coming to understand that having one's parents *in situ* is not a condition necessary to being a middle-aged child. One is always a child. The first hint of this I had was at the funeral of an elderly man. He was eulogized fondly by several friends and clergy, all of whom referred to his three sons—themselves well into middle age—as "the Brown boys." That was three years ago, and they are still known collectively as "the Brown boys," even though they are themselves nearing retirement.

If the world at large sometimes identifies us by our parents (and, at the other end of the generational ladder, by our children), in our interior world there is no escaping our parents' legacy. Alive or dead, their voices resonate in our heads, guiding us, admonishing us. We all know people who are living out their parents' expectations for them in careers not necessarily of their own choosing, in jobs they no longer fully enjoy, striving for the success and recognition they feel their parents expect (expected) of them. Those are deep-seated patterns of behavior, long-established lifestyles. They take energy and courage to change. But relatively insignificant social conduct is no less difficult to alter, it seems. "It's been four years since my mother died, and I still write thank-you notes to my hostess the morning after a dinner party," says a woman I know. "It isn't because that is a polite thing to do—I just thanked her ten hours earlier—but because I constantly hear my mother reminding me about good manners." Jules Feiffer caught the generational crossfire in *Grown Ups,* in two lines of conversation between the play's hero and his sister as they discuss their parents' aggravating behavior.

Sister: I could kill them.

Brother: That would only be a short-term solution.

Long-term solutions are what we are after: that perfect state of grace wherein we have made our peace with our parents, ourselves, our children, and are functioning as caring adults who accord dignity and respect to our elders and our youngers. This demands hard work, harder than many of us are able—or perhaps willing—to perform. It starts with patience and humor and nonjudgmental support (everything we expect of practically everybody else), and it requires close attention and understanding, what Theodor Reik called listening with the third ear. There is also the actuarial imperative, and now more than ever we have to listen for what our parents really want—not for what we want to hear but for what they are really saying. It's an exercise in aural translation, and some people are better at languages than others.

For instance, here is my mother sitting across a café table from me, sipping a glass of wine. In answer to my guilt-ridden explanation, she is saying, with an absolutely straight face, "I know you're busy writing, Joan. Of course, I understand that it's hard for you to visit." Can I believe her? Of course not. But how seductive the words are. If I accept her assertion at face value, it will be not only because that pleases me but also because I want to think that pleases her. Which is not to say that my own guilt machine won't make something of it.

My father, on the other hand, doesn't have such seemingly reassuring conversations. Like many men in their seventies and eighties, his moods tilt between crankily self-absorbed and awesomely feisty. Ever since he closed his law office—at age eighty-three, no longer willing to sign three-year leases—he has been impatient, testy. Still sharp as ever, crusty as rye, too cold in winter, too warm in summer, angry at being in his eighties, angry at not having destinations and purposes.

Here is a man fighting for his life. When my mother broke her arm and couldn't toast his English muffins or broil his fish, he wouldn't accept help from me.

"Get out of the kitchen," he orders, his bony fingers pushing me out the door.

"It's only a cup of tea," I protest.

"Never mind," he says. "I can make it."

The wonder is not that he can make a cup of tea for himself but that he knows where the kitchen is at all because for all his eighty-five years women have been making his tea and his muffins, his hot chocolate and his scrambled eggs. It never symbolized helplessness before.

"Oh, God," I wail to my husband when I get home. "My father!"

"Isn't it wonderful," says Rafe. "Look at that spirit! Would you rather have him passive and accepting? Be glad he's still fighting."

What looks like fight in our aging parents is usually fear, De-Berry explains. "Often the anxiety over increased sickness and dependency causes the older adult to overreact, to withdraw into a shell of pseudo-independence or self-assertion. To become irritable, yet to refuse any attempt at intervention. Not to want to be a bother."

Shows of independence are common among the elders of my friends. Josie's father, frail and virtually housebound, will not allow anyone to prepare his meals for him. Carol's aunt, despite severe cataracts and frequently mending bones, stumbles to her neighborhood patisserie for her daily sweet. Some acts of self-sufficiency are to be applauded, some are bewildering, others are so confounding that third ears—and fourth and fifth—are not likely to perceive underlying emotions. For instance, every so often I have a circular conversation with my father that leaves me wondering if my two actual ears are functioning properly. Here is a typical exchange:

"I want to move," says my father, "so I can go to a club and be by myself." He has a club where he is. Moving means something else.

"So go to your club and play cards. Or take a walk in the park."

"She"—not even "Your mother"—"she always wants to walk with me." Actually, my mother gives him fairly long reins, and when they're together, they are always hand in hand. His idea. They are devoted, each the other's best friend, and since he has given up his office, they are virtually inseparable. In the domestic arena, she is the doer, the planner, the instigator. He is the follower. When my mother goes to Italian class, my father walks with her. My mother goes marketing, my father walks with her. My mother takes a walk, my father takes a walk.

"Let's get this straight," he says, as if to a dim-witted client. "Your mother is the most wonderful person in the world and I love her more than anyone I've ever loved in the world. But I need to be by myself."

"So be by yourself. Take a walk."

"Then she wants to walk with me."

When the weather turns cold, he offers a variation on the same theme. "I have to get out of New York in the winter," he says. "I hate it."

"What are you going to do?"

"I'm going to sell the apartment and move someplace warm."

"Does Mother know?" I'm not worried; the apartment is not subject to an impetuous or hasty sale.

"No, she doesn't," he says gruffly. "And if she doesn't like it, I'll go without her."

I don't answer.

"You'll see," he threatens. "She can come and live with you."

Cranky independence has its flip side, and when our parents redirect the psychic energy that fuels their fears and anxieties, their vitality and accomplishments are exhilarating and sometimes astonishing. My friend Dick describes his father and the cave of bats. When his father was seventy-one, the extended family took a trip to the Yucatán. The day they visited a burial site in a cave outside Chichén Itzá was particularly oppressive and hot. The route through an airless passage was narrow and low, part of it accessible only by crawling on hands and knees. Bats thronged the dark passageway. At one point his father, who was usually in the front of the group, dropped back and sat on a rock.

"I can't go on," he said.

When the guide assured him the burial site was only a hundred yards ahead, his father jumped up, renewed, and completed the crawl.

"I admire the ability of my father to say he couldn't make it," says Dick proudly, "and then that wonderful resurgence of energy to do it."

The same sense of vitality often energizes my father, and he and my mother strike out on an adventure that is awesome in its breadth for octogenarians, let alone for anyone thirty or forty years younger. They plan a trip to China, and instantly they seem to have shed fifteen years. They go to lectures on the arts of China, the ancient customs, the contemporary life, the folkways. They hang out at the China Institute. They enroll in a Chinese language course at a local college. Every morning from 8:00 to 11:00 they are in class, studying the ideograms, the phrases. Then, hand, in hand, they walk home for lunch, haltingly trying out new phrases.

"Nǐ hǎo ma?"

"Xièxie nǐ, hen-hǎo."

Suddenly life has purpose and meaning. Moreover, my father would get an A from Levinson; he is meeting the principal task of an old man: "to sustain his youthfulness in a new form appropriate to late adulthood . . . [retaining the] connection to youthful vitality, to the forces of growth in self and world." My parents revel in their vitality and activeness. They are exuberantly proud of their accomplishments. They are not only splendid role models, they are exemplars of what Neugarten calls "the young-old," the elderly who are mentally and physically vigorous, and are helping to shape what she calls an "age-irrelevant society."

"We had a wonderful day in class," my mother reports one day. The professor, charmed with the octogenarian couple, has taken the time to elicit some personal history. On this particular day, he announces to the class that it is their fifty-ninth wedding anniversary. The class applauded and, rising to thank their young classmates, my mother coyly explained she was "a Kentucky bride of nine." "I didn't want them to figure out my age," she confessed later.

Sometimes, however, that feisty spirit can get out of hand. Two years ago, for instance, when my father was eighty-three, he mapped a trip by car from Rome to Barcelona. My father hasn't been at the wheel of a car in the United States for sixteen years, but he keeps his driver's license current; my mother hasn't driven in decades. Appalled at his plan, I raised all the obvious objections: What will you do if you get sick on a country road? If you have car trouble in the middle of nowhere? When the Porsches zoom by at 140 miles per hour? I didn't mention my recurring vision of them plunging from the Grande Corniche into the Mediterranean. My ordinarily sensible mother said, "We'll be perfectly all right. We're not going to drive more than a hundred miles a day."

To my relief, the trip didn't materialize for other reasons, but the next year, there he was, poring over the same Michelin maps. This time, having spent some months thinking about parents and children, getting older, and the quality of life (and perhaps betraying my own middle-aged guilt and ambivalence), I thought, Well, why not? It's not a bad way to go. I just hope to hell no one else is on the road.

Capricious parental behavior is familiar to most of my friends. Marie, for instance, frequently invites her mother for the weekend. Her mother has been visiting her for twenty years. One day, her mother announced, "I'm not going to make the trip again." No warning. No explanation. "If you want to see me, you can make the trip." Marie, who always listens with a third ear, has by now figured out what her mother was really saying, but at the time she sighed and said, "When we're old, let's not be as crazy as our parents."

That would be nice (especially for our children) but I suspect that if we're not careful, of course we will be. What's more, if that old saw is correct about seeing our future selves in our parents, we can foretell just how crazy we are apt to be, and in precisely what ways. Am I likely to be an incorrigible crank tearing around country roads? (Probably.) A long-suffering mother waiting for a son to call? (Not bloody likely.) A peppy octogenarian studying Mycenaean culture? (I hope so.)

Actually, students of family life tell us that as we grow older, rather than ape our parents, we will fall back on our own past histories (which reflect plenty of parental influence). Florence Shelley predicts that good relationships will get better, poor ones get worse. "Character is extremely consistent," says DeBerry. "The single most reliable factor for predicting one's future behavior is one's behavior in the present." However we turn out in our own older age, we'll have no one to blame but ourselves.

What we can foresee from the complicated business of being a middle-aged child, and a parent of a middle-aged child, is that we'll have a better shot at a lively and vital old age of our own if we work out our family relationships while we are still in the middle of that continuum. Enlightened self-interest is a powerful energizer. It should prompt us to come to terms with how to act our age, how to function as the middle generation. When we master that ever-present age dilemma, we'll find it easier to be more understanding of our children and more compassionate of our elders. We ought to—if only to create a history of our own that we will want to rely on in the future.

12

LEARNING TO LIVE WITH IT

The last time I took my aching back to the orthopedist, I expected a cure along with the fancy bill. After all, I had brought similar ailments to him before, and the results of his ministrations had always been therapeutic. In time, the tennis elbow improved (but not the backhand that caused it). The broken toe healed, the torn ligament mended. I had every reason to expect that the back would respond to medical attention as well. So I was totally unprepared for the diagnosis: "General wear and tear on the spinal joints. Just learn to live with it."

Actually, this wasn't the first time I had heard that advice. When I was forty (and practically the day after my birthday had to get my first pair of bifocals) I complained to the eye doctor about these new spots that were floating around in my eyes.

"Don't give it another thought," he said cavalierly, just as I was warming up to a full recitation of my symptoms. "We call them floaters. They come with middle age."

I promptly dismissed the eye doctor and took my spots to another ophthalmologist who was gentleman enough not to remind me why various parts of the body were wearing out. It was the classic ploy of killing the messenger who brings bad news. The second eye doctor was very sympathetic. He assured me that *lots* of people had floaters, and while he didn't exactly say there was a high incidence among toddlers, neither did he tie it to any aging process. (Another messenger who bit the dust for the same reason was the gynecologist who told a thirty-eight-year-old friend that she needn't worry about long-term effects from using the pill since, at her age, menopause was imminent anyway.)

The most depressing part of the orthopedist's advice was that

I was prepared to take it. There wasn't any point in dismissing this messenger; at my age all the other bearers of tidings would doubtless carry the same bad news. Being middle-aged is learning that things are only going to get worse. And probably all at the same time.

"A number of changes commonly occurring at around 40 intensify the sense of aging," writes Levinson, profiling the physical state of his middle-aged Everyman. "He cannot run as fast, lift as much, do with as little sleep as before. His vision and hearing are less acute, he remembers less well and finds it harder to learn masses of specific information." And as if that isn't enough, he hasn't even started on serious illnesses. As a friend of mine said recently, "Don't give me your aching back. My sister-in-law is bleeding internally, we're having two people with cancer for dinner, my husband's partner had a fatal heart attack—and the good news is that he died in his sleep." What was once untimely, premature, is now, if not timely, at least not surprising. What used to shock us is now coming into sync with what Neugarten calls "a sense of the life cycle: an anticipation and acceptance of the inevitable sequence of events that occur as men grow up, grow old, and die." Being middle-aged is learning to live with it.

Of course, learning to live with it implies being able to live with it, which is a good deal better than not being able to. And, putting aside the discomfort, indeed pain, that may attend our various conditions, what seems to me a different kind of burden is the frustrating lack of control, the irritating inability to retain mastery over our bodies. Our chronic afflictions can no longer be repaired. There's not a damn thing we can do about it. *Just learn to live with it.*

One principal frustration, for me, at least, is the matter of forgetfulness. (That has a nice dispassionate judicial ring to it—In the matter of *forgetfulness v. Scobey*—intended to defuse the despair attached to this irritating loss of memory and suggesting that maybe the verdict isn't in after all. I may be losing my memory but not my ability to fool myself.) More and more I find myself unable to put my tongue around some word that is essential to my sentence. I don't mean the name of a cousin whom I haven't seen in years, which I regard tolerantly as an understandable lapse. Nor do I expect to recall the name of a charming town in France, even though

Rafe and I thought we might like to spend the rest of our lives there. It isn't even that the name of my husband eludes me in moments of social panic. ("Marv," I say to a high school classmate Rafe and I have run into on the street, "I'd like you to meet . . . ummm . . . errr . . . my husband.")

More often than not I am stopped midsentence by the absence of a perfectly simple word. The other day I was telling Carol about a book I was reading, and I was trying to describe the author's style.

"In practically every sentence, there are words that are, um, you know, like, underlined," I start to explain. "And then to be sure we get the point, there's a sentence in parentheses that always ends in a . . . uh . . . that long thin line with a dot at the bottom."

"Exclamation point?" asks Carol. "You mean italicized words and exclamation points?"

Yes.

Most of the time it's not as bad as that. Usually it's a name or place I don't really expect to keep at the top of my head. The other evening, for instance, Rafe was telling friends about a restaurant he particularly likes. He couldn't remember the name. He doesn't mumble and stutter around. He simply turns to me. (When he's in his office, he turns to his secretary; he doesn't require an elaborate retrieval system.)

"Joan, what's the name of that restaurant we like near the Metropolitan Museum?"

I know which one he means, but only because we have been married for twenty-eight years. The restaurant is nowhere near the Met, but we once had a memorable dinner there after seeing a Monet show at the museum.

"You mean . . . it's . . ." I slap my hand to forehead in what is becoming a frequent gesture of despair. "Oh, God! What is the name?"

Our companions smile understandingly. Nodding, they say, "Thank goodness it happens to other people!"

"No, no," I say. "I'll have it in a minute. It starts with Chez and the owner has another restaurant in the sixties that starts with Bistro and his first name is Robert, and they put *saucisson en croûte* on the table as soon as you sit down, and . . ."

But no name. I have several other identifying details, like the brick walls and the pink lighting, but nothing that would ever lead anyone to enjoy a meal at the place.

Carol, who admits to more than her share of forgetting, says she has a distinct picture of her mental retrieval system. "There are a lot of files in my head. Everything I know is filed up there, waiting to be recalled. When I need to know something, a hand reaches in there to get it. Only the hand is so limp that it can't grasp the information."

I don't have the same image. My visualized retrieval mechanism is much more automated than Carol's. As a matter of fact, my files are probably better organized, as she would be the first to admit. I am extremely well organized, which makes my increasingly frequent memory lapses particularly galling. For instance, I know that this restaurant I'm trying to remember is listed both alphabetically and geographically in my mental files. Also by quality. So by rights I should have several routes to reclaim the data. When I push the Select button, I visualize the scanner moving rapidly past the *A*s and *B*s into the *Chez* listings. Then shifting to the Upper East Side listings. Then to the Three Star category. All this, I imagine, is practically instantaneous. No limp and floppy hands poking their damp fingers into my gray files. A crisp electronic recovery of stored information. But somewhere in that instant, the circuitry shorts out, the storage disks crash, everything shuts down.

Help!

Perhaps I am not yet ready for such advanced technology. Like the Peter Principle, I have elevated my memory retrieval far above its capability. I should retreat to simpler technology. Employ visual aids ("When the little hand is on three and the big hand is on six, it's half past . . .") and three-by-five cards. Real three-by-five cards you can lay your hands on, that keep all high-priority data literally at your fingertips (if you're home and near the file). Keep efficient lists. Devise mnemonic devices as our local fish store did; it advertises its telephone number as 725-FISH. Or the man I know who remembers a friend's phone number as HOT-TIME. (Not to be confused with the Chevy owner who sports the same two words on his license plate.)

And concentrate hard. Here the difficulty is that you must focus on everything, since you never know exactly what information you might want to recall. Moreover, you are likely to relax in familiar settings. Such as when you start out for the living room to get the Sunday crossword puzzle and the pencil in your pocketbook, and you arrive in the living room remembering only that the trip had something to do with your pocketbook (which isn't there anyway). "Let's see, what did I come in here for" and "Oh, dear, what did I do with it" run a close second in our house to "What the devil is the name of that place (person, thing)."

Just as I was considering other ways of coping, my friend Bob the golfer told me this story about some familiar chronic ailments, and eventually learning to live with them. He swears it's true. Eighty-six-year-old Sam is complaining to his doctor that he can't play golf anymore.

"Nonsense," says the doctor. "You're in perfect health. Just go out and play."

"But I can't see the ball anymore," says Sam. "When I hit it, I can't see where it goes."

"You should play with Ben. He'll watch the ball for you."

"Ben? He's ninety-two!"

"But he has perfect eyesight. Sees like an eagle. The two of you would do well together."

So Sam and Ben go out to the first hole. Sam steps up to the tee and hits his drive.

"I see it," cries Ben. "There it goes . . . it's still going . . . past the one-hundred-and-fifty-yard marker . . . now it's bouncing on the fairway . . . it's by a rough."

"Good," says Sam, as they walk down the fairway toward the ball. "Now where is it?"

"I forget."

The only comforting aspect of midstream forgetfulness is that it's so widely shared. I assume it isn't early senility, or the medical journals would be alerting the population to a mid-life epidemic. But what is it? A woman I hadn't seen since high school offered a diagnosis as we were trying to recall the names of some class-mates, and having the predictable frustrations: transient cerebral ischemia. She had heard this from a friend, and was so gratified to have the affliction designated—especially its transient aspect—that she wrote it down on a piece of paper and keeps it on her refrigerator door, next to all the other important reminders of her current life.

Because I don't necessarily rely on middle-aged women who practice medicine without a license, I checked further into the mysterious ways that memory works and, more and more often, fails to. This is a puzzle that continues to baffle scientists, but recent research suggests that the process may have a biochemical as well as psychological component. It also has a physiological basis. As our aging brains gradually lose cells, they are slower to process information, react to it, and retrieve it. Small memory lapses may be just an overload of facts in our mental databases. And although our response time is slowing, our intelligence is not, I was relieved to learn from the National Institute of Aging studies.

When I queried our gray-haired family doctor, he took the evolutionary view. "One of the things that happens in middle age is that some parts of the body just wear out," he explained. "You know, in the beginning we weren't designed to live past thirty or forty."

Most of us do (even if our brain cells and a joint or two lag behind), but along the way there is often serious sickness. And nothing is guaranteed to revive our anxieties about our own mortality like a bout with a life-threatening illness. The experience can be very much like a death, as I learned from a close friend. She had a mastectomy, and under the circumstances, all reports were good: no affected nodes, no need for chemotherapy, no further treatment of any kind. She quickly returned to work, feeling good about the prognosis and about her future. Fairly soon she was having dark dreams every night, and a heavy gray depression rolled in. "I worked even harder," she said, "but it didn't help."

"Keeping busy" is always prescribed for the bad times. It is meant to divert us, keep us on track, propel us forward. But to family therapist Elliott Rosen it is a myth that you have to get on with life after a loss. "No," he says, "you should face it, cope with it first. You can't get on with life by avoiding the loss or trauma."

My friend was wise enough to seek help, and to realize that she was indeed avoiding a confrontation with the trauma of having cancer. In fact, she came to understand that she actually was in mourning, albeit for the loss of a breast and all that it represents to women. For several days she lay in her darkened room, not fighting the despondency, giving her melancholia its due. And then, as if a fever broke, she emerged from her depression. As she recounts the emotional passage, her eyes glint. "And it didn't help me one bit," she said, laughing, "that in the middle of all this an entrepreneurial undertaker called to tell me I had been selected to receive a free burial plot."

Of all mid-life conditions, chronic or acute, timely or untimely, appropriate or wildly unexpected, the most difficult to make peace with is surely the deaths of those we love. Let's start with parents, only because in the life cycle their deaths are least unexpected. (Did you notice the excessive negatives in that last sentence?) The death of our parents is so unacceptable that we often tend to reject the whole concept. My own father, as I've mentioned, is eighty-five years old. Any rational child of his would accept that he is in his last years—golden, sunset, whatever the euphemism. Somewhere in the deep folds of my (un)conscious mind, however, I like to believe that he has stumbled onto a fountain of youth. That this man who lives in the heart of urban America and not in the mountains of the Georgian Republic of the USSR, who eats pickles and ham sandwiches not yogurt, has somehow found the key to immortality. And if he's found it, then (a) he is still at the head of the generational line, running interference for me; and (b) he will certainly share his magic secret with me.

You may suspect that I haven't exactly come to terms with the idea of my parents' dying. What's more, I am not alone. "All our life we've feared losing our parents," says Gould. "When our parents die, the fear of our own death becomes exaggerated . . . now that they are gone, we are next—and it can happen at any time. If one parent is still alive, we can maintain the illusion that death is an orderly event which we are protected against by someone else."

The death of the remaining parent is truly traumatic; it strips us of our last defense. My friend Pam remembers blurting out after her mother died, "I feel so alone." Elliott Rosen recalls, "As I walked back from my father's grave site, I felt: I am the man. He's gone. I have to take care of myself."

How we make peace with the death of our parents depends, naturally, on what has gone before in the relationship. Some people can't easily tolerate the idea that their parents are no longer around to observe their success; others are relieved they can't witness their failures. Almost everyone feels that, whatever the history or circumstances, the moment has come just a little too soon, cutting off forever our chance to say what we have left unsaid.

The death of a spouse escalates the trauma and vulnerability in geometric proportions, not to mention the loneliness, terror, and insecurity it adds. It is unimaginable to me. (What I mean is that it is terrifyingly imaginable; I simply choose not to imagine it.) The ache, and the loss, and the loneliness—a battalion of chichés march to mind and I'm willing to let them stand. The idea of Rafe's dying is so horrifying that I won't spend time shaping the anguish into more intimate phrases. Ache, loss, loneliness is a good beginning. This is why, I suppose, the language of the obituary page is so formalized: beloved husband, loving mother, adored sister, devoted child. Commercial locutions dropped into every death notice, but to each of the bereaved sentiments well and truly writ. Yes, that obituese would fit: beloved husband, loving father, adored brother, devoted son. Just for a start. And just for the public occasion.

One day Rick inadvertently tapped into a dark private abyss when he asked, "What happens when Dad dies?" What popped out of my mouth was, "I'm going to be mad as hell." I am. I am going to be furious at his unexcused absence. At being abandoned. At his leaving me in the lurch. I am going to be one angry widow. (I'm not at all sure he will feel the same way, but if I go first, I hope he has the good taste not to settle down with anyone younger or thinner than me.)

What little I know of widowhood comes from two close friends. Both husbands dropped dead of heart attacks, one over his office desk, the other never got up one morning. There was no time for leave-taking, good-byes, anything. One minute you're a wife, the next you're a widow. And in Carol's case, a childless widow. Moreover, they were not only widowed unexpectedly, they were widowed before they thought to prepare for it. There was no "rehearsal for widowhood," as Neugarten calls the period in which "the events are anticipated and rehearsed, the grief work completed, the reconciliation accomplished without shattering the sense of continuity of the life cycle."

Carol recalls the day seven years ago when her husband's colleague called with the news. "I kept trying to remember—what was the last thing I said to him." Her anguished need to know how she and Buddy parted was profoundly affecting. Ever since, I have tried to make sure that I won't be caught feeling sorry for the things I have said (or not said). And when I have behaved with typical ill temper, one superstitious corner of my mind keeps my verbal insurance policy up to date by silently flashing the appropriate message as Rafe goes off on his appointed rounds: *ListenIshouldn'thaveyelledaboutthedirtydishesYouknowIloveyoulikecrazy.*

For Sue Ellen, widowed eight months ago, the shock is still fresh, raw. And painfully connected to her own sense of aging. "I felt older immediately," she says. "I looked in the mirror the next day and I couldn't believe it—I had aged ten years. A recently widowed friend said that was because there isn't a man around to tell you that you still look gorgeous. And in a way that's true. I can't feel like his child bride anymore." Her eyes misted as she relived the first months. "I sometimes do crazy things. I've broken at least a dozen crystal glasses. I get hot and cold flushes that my doctor says are due to the trauma. I feel like my hormonal system is out of kilter." Her pause underscored the obvious: her whole life is out of kilter. She seemed to need to talk about it.

"The worst time is in the morning, when you wake up alone. I can manage the twilight hours. I don't sit down and have a drink, like we used to—I find all kinds of tasks that must be done, weeding the garden, cleaning a closet. I think that's why widows are always fussing around their homes. It's not so hard when you're up and doing things."

Sue Ellen is seeking refuge in the "keeping busy" syndrome. Perhaps that—plus her openness in talking about feelings—will help her make peace with her widowhood. How else to confront it? By driving down an isolated country road, stopping the car, and primally screaming? By moaning in bed, "No . . . no . . . no . . ." until the sobs finally turn into a whispered, "Yes?" By having a solitary cocktail and saying to the empty chair, "You aren't here. You never will be again. I have to learn to enjoy a glass of wine alone now. Cheers?"

People come to terms with death in their own private ways.

Carol seemed stupefied, almost dazed, to be widowed and childless. Despite the ministrations of many caring friends, it was a long time before the sparkle returned, before, as she says, "The juices started flowing again." The wonder was that they ever did. And when they did, her appetite for living seemed greater, her zest for adventure keener, her feeling for people more compassionate. On one of our vacations together, we ran into a man she hadn't seen in ten years.

"Catch me up with your news," he said eagerly. "How's Buddy? Where is your daughter?"

"Well, Buddy died three years ago, and Kathy five years earlier."

He was stunned, embarassed at having asked.

"I really zapped you," she said with a smile, trying to put him at ease. Later she said to me, "Poor guy, I felt terrible for him. He was only being polite. I hate to lay a heavy load like that on anyone, but I just don't know what else to say."

Carol completed her graduate studies in social work, wryly noting that chance had provided more "life experience" credentials than a good social worker really needs. She now has a hospital position, a full professional career, but even after seven years, she occasionally drives to the cemetery and shakes her fist at her husband's grave.

Sue Ellen is still inching her way back to a solitary life. Until a year before Walt's death she was a full-time journalist; he had retired early to enjoy his cooking, his music, his home. There was a piquant role reversal in their professional lives, and now his death has nudged her into a more traditional role. "In some ways I've taken over Walt's life," she observes. "I do the marketing and plan the meals, things I never did or liked to do. And I find myself thinking, Walt enjoyed doing this. I enjoy doing this." Having a son nearby who comes for weekends eases the transition. "Just to make two cups of coffee in the morning . . . roll up a pair of men's socks . . . iron his handkerchiefs . . ."

Whether you have to learn about life insurance and annuities, or whether, like Sue Ellen, you are first finding out that frozen turkey is cheaper than fresh, living without a spouse obviously entails fundamental changes. Not all of them turn out to be bad. Sue Ellen reports a blossoming of friendships with other women. "Not

126

just widows," she says. "Sometimes it's like a sorority." Female bonding, younger women call it. When husbands are widowed, I'm not sure that they turn to male bonding. However they deal with their grief privately, publicly they also seem to embrace female friendships.

One surprise is that so many women like not being responsible for anyone else. "It's different when you no longer share a room, a bathroom," says Sue Ellen. "I've rearranged our room now, put things in different places." Not Carol. She has barely moved anything. She still sleeps on her side of the bed. But she points out the compensations of widowhood that help in learning to live without a husband:

1. Not having to open the bedroom window at night.

2. Not having to think about dinner. Or endure the guilt of serving tuna fish more than once a week.

3. No more Super Sundays.

"The main advantage is the chance to be utterly selfish. To plan only for me. To eat when I want to, sleep when I want to, read until three in the morning if I want to. There is only myself to take care of."

Carol, who comes from a time when married couples were regulation issue, is not at all surprised at how many widows won't marry again just for the sake of getting married. What did surprise her was to discover parts of herself she never knew existed, a willingness to live in very different ways. "Since Bud died, I've learned that in spite of profound personal loss, one goes on. Life is not the same, but it can still be fun."

Carol is one of the great survivors. She gives me hope that the rest of us can make it, too. In *Hour of Gold, Hour of Lead,* Anne Morrow Lindbergh illuminates her own survival: "It is as if the intensity of grief fused the distance between you and the dead. Or perhaps, in reality, part of one dies. If one is lucky, one is reborn. . . . Some people die and are reborn many times in their lives. For others the ground is too barren and the time too short for rebirth." Perhaps learning to live with our human condition is making sure that our soil is always fertile enough to sustain whatever rebirths may be necessary.

13

COMING
OF AGE

When the questionnaire heralding my thirtieth college reunion arrived, it not only reminded me that I was no longer twenty-seven, it also called into review the quality of those last thirty years.

Are you still married to your first husband? (Yes.)

Has your political center of gravity shifted? (No.)

Have you developed new skills or interests for leisure time? (No. Still tennis, travel, writing, family. Not necessarily in that order.)

What kinds of communities have you lived in? (Same suburban town.)

By the time I got to the domicile question, I saw a dismaying pattern. Even the same house, for God's sake! Nothing substantive had changed. A little thinner, a new vocabulary that included "cellulite" and "actuarial imperative." But still, a depressing sameness to the story. Was this continuity or stagnation? (A classmate had a complementary reaction to the same questionnaire. Her responses indicated so much change—of husbands, expertise, living arrangements and places—that she wondered if her life bespoke adventure or instability.)

My pursuit of Big Answers to large life-assessing questions was unwittingly accelerated shortly thereafter when I was driving a familiar (naturally!) route from supermarket to home. I turned the corner and found myself caught in the middle of a funeral procession, five cars back from the hearse. It was noon of a sunny day. All the headlights were on. Until I could leave the procession at the next corner, I was part of this funeral cortege.

As I get older, I'm increasingly attuned to symbols, especially of mortality. And this one didn't escape me. Was God telling me to get my house in order? Which one? The gray clapboard with the crabgrass or the gray cells with the crabby temper? Or simply to pay closer attention when I drive? I also notice I'm not the only one in mid-life observing mortality symbols. A friend who had to replace her eighteen-year-old bedsprings was jolted by the realization that she was probably buying her last mattress. Having recently survived a bout with cancer, she said poignantly, "I'll be glad to get eighteen years out of it." My editor friend Tom, on the other hand, is already prepared for a similar situation in outlasting one's possessions. "When the dog dies," he said, sensing there would be time for only one more canine acquisition, "I'm not going to replace him. I want to be the survivor."

Tom and his dog, Lynn and her mattress, I and the funeral cortege neatly tie up several strands that developmental theorists identify with mid-life *angst:* life-threatening illness, confrontation with death (albeit one's dog or an anonymous body), and a shift in time perception to "time left to live." As Levinson notes, "The emphasis gradually shifts from past to future." We increasingly realize that the future is finite; worse yet, it's practically here.

We've already witnessed (if not experienced) how the press of time provokes all kinds of behavior: panicky flights into sexual adventures, hysteria at the health spa, second careers and second wives, not to mention foolhardy as well as courageous risk taking. But there does seem to be a point at which the thrashing around subsides into a more reflective mode. We sense that it's time to pause, to stand back from the action and appraise it.

Curiously, this half-time intermission seemingly occurs without our conscious help. Even the least reflective among us grope for some self-understanding at this midpassage. From studies of mid-life men and women, Neugarten notes, "We are impressed with reflection as a striking characteristic of the mental life of middle-aged persons: the stocktaking, the heightened introspection, and, above all, the structuring and restructuring of experience." What have we learned? Have we done what we wanted to? Have we done it the way we wanted to?

For all but the most self-satisfied, the answers are likely to disappoint. Introspection is a risky business. Asking questions permits unsatisfactory answers. As novelist James Baldwin observes, "Between what one wishes to become and what one *has* become there is a momentous gap, which will now never be closed. . . . Some of us are compelled, around the middle of our lives, to make a study of this baffling geography, less in the hope of conquering these distances than in the determination that the distance shall not become any greater."

If we are determined to hold the line—or, more optimistically, narrow the gap—we have to face the demons that are driving us. Moreover, we have to accept them. And for many of us there is a long agenda in need of forgiveness.

To start with, there is the disparity that Baldwin notes between what we are—whatever that may be—and what we would be. This is a delicate assessment, entirely personal; a gap may not be apparent to anyone else at all. We must confront our own dragons and exorcise them. We must learn to forget our missed chances, forgive our poor choices, accept our frail selves. And in so doing, we may still the ghosts and whispers of our parents who, we think, want more and other things of us, and the expectations of our spouses. By forgiving ourselves, we will be able to forgive others.

Of this half-time assessment, Gould says, "sometime in our forties decade . . . we step from the intense heat of the mid-life period to a cooled-down, post-mid-life attitude. We live with a sense of having completed something, a sense that we are whoever we are going to be—and we accept that, not with resignation to the negative feeling that we could have been more and have failed, but with a more positive acceptance. Here I am! This is me!"

In truth, the sooner we accept our life's choices, the easier our passage, as my friend Elena discovered. "I feel that some kind of deep transformation that has been incubating within me for several years has finally reached a plateau, perhaps only a temporarily stable point, but a very welcome one nonetheless," she wrote me on becoming forty. "I feel suddenly much more free because, in part, I have fully understood and accepted the choices that I *have* made over the years. How embarrassing if this is not the sign of a mature woman happily entering middle age but rather of a belated and painful tearing away from adolescence! Ah well, whatever it is, I'm much more comfortable on this side of it!"

Because accepting ourselves gracefully is rare, I am inclined to collect testimonials to middle age. Joanne Woodward, for instance, was past fifty when she said, "Before the age of forty-five my life was a disaster. I'm the only person I know who enjoys growing old." Actually, she isn't alone. Beverly Sills, who describes herself as being in her "dessert days," said, "I really cherish being fifty, and I kind of like the serenity that comes with it." (Among the many reasons that Beverly Sills is a role model of mine is her delight in the best part of a meal.) Of course, everything is relative, and it's comparatively easy to accept growing old when you're fifty and there is still lots of time to do it. Then again, maybe it even gets easier; as Maurice Chevalier said on happily reaching eighty, "Consider the alternative."

Moreover, once we make peace with our age, we are apt to find that we will worry far less about what others think of us and more about what we think of ourselves. Not only will we hear our own internal voices more clearly, but we will attend them more closely. Giving up the need to have our choices approved—let alone determined—by others is one of the great comforts of growing old. As my friend Ginny says, "At last we can indulge our eccentricities, even make fools of ourselves."

What Ginny calls eccentricity, adult developmentalists are apt to call "individuation." "Individuation is a developmental process through which a person becomes more uniquely individual," explains Levinson. "Acquiring a clearer and fuller identity of his own, he becomes better able to utilize his inner resources and pursue his own aims. . . ." Individuation is what lets us say, *Here I am! This is me!*

Keep in mind that the me you're blessing is also the one with the body that's betraying you at every turn, the one with the lagging memory and the sagging muscles and the flagging reflexes. We accept ourselves biologically, and that includes our physical limitations, even—God help us—our appearance. (Although I don't know that I'd go as far as our son David, the historian, who says, "A face without wrinkles has no history written on it.") Once we begin to accept ourselves, there's no point in going halfway. We forgive ourselves wholeheartedly, as a debt is forgiven: the whole sum, not just one or two installments.

However, coming to terms with growing old is infinitely easier than the next challenge: accepting the inevitability of death. Of one's own death. The irony is that our mid-life years are characterized by anxiety over just that certainty. Intimations of mortality are precisely what fuel our mid-life infernos. Is this really all there is to the Grand Design? Even if we believe that every day is all there is, we can't help hoping for more. As Woody Allen said, "I don't believe in an afterlife, although I am bringing a change of underwear."

Recognizing that one's own death is inevitable is a far cry from accepting it. Most theorists of adult development see this as a prime task of the mid-life years. Erik Erikson calls this ultimate stage ego integrity. It indicates not only acceptance of the quality of one's life but also of its foreseeable end. "The lack or loss of this accrued ego integration is signified by fear of death: the one and only life cycle is not accepted as the ultimate of life," he writes. "Despair expresses the feeling that the time is now short, too short for the attempt to start another life and to try out alternate roads to integrity."

Once we begin to overcome our fear of death, to confront the inevitability of our own finale, the roads to integrity that looked so thorny now seem remarkably free of underbrush. This doesn't mean we abandon our dreams of immortality. "On the contrary," Levinson assures us, "this wish becomes more conscious, more subject to reflective thought, more modest and realistic in its aims." By scaling down our expectations and narrowing our goals, we may even find that different, if less grandiose, delights await us.

"The afternoon of life" is what Anne Morrow Lindbergh calls this particular pleasure in *Gift From the Sea*. "We Americans, with our terrific emphasis on youth, action, and material success, certainly tend to belittle the afternoon of life and even to pretend it never comes. We push the clock back and try to prolong the morning, over-reaching and overstraining ourselves in the unnatural effort. We do not succeed, of course. . . . In our breathless attempts we often miss the flowering that waits for afternoon."

With fewer daylight hours to savor, how shall we spend them? The obvious answer is, Very carefully. But how?

What comes to mind is the concept of triage. Triage is the process of grading by quality. It started with coffee beans and was drafted in wartime by medical units to assign treatment in short supply to those with the greatest chance of survival. Triage has possibilities in mid-life as well: to sort out and select the most fulfilling activities and engaging pursuits for our limited time and diminishing energies.

I anticipated that Ultimate Selections would be hard, but the things I want to do—and those I want to avoid—bubble up readily. To paraphrase Samuel Johnson, the prospect of limited time concentrates the mind wonderfully.

We have been making choices all our adult lives, but with Ultimate Selections there seem to be significant differences. For one thing, style as well as substance seems increasingly important. Roads are coming to have at least as much meaning as destinations. What we are going to do is often less important than how we will do it. Process counts. Perhaps that's why my How List is a lot longer than the What List.

This is not to say that I don't have a few concrete aims in mind. Every winter there is this recurring fantasy: I will dust off my forty-year-old copy of Czerny's *Art of Finger Dexterity,* set the metronome a-ticking, and practice my piano so that someday soon I can dazzle myself (and a few friends) with a Mozart sonata. My summer fantasy is in French. Or Italian. Or Spanish. We are foreign residents (short-term probably, definitely not tourists), and I speak—and dream—in a flawless native tongue. As my friend Barbara says, "I want to speak the local language so the natives don't answer me in English." Tucked in between my intransitive verbs and intractable scales I want to write a detective story.

My friends have similar dreams. Laurie wants to spend time with poetry. "I want to hear it, understand its wisdom," she says. Nancy wants time for daydreaming. "Middle-aged people are hooked on being productive," she says. "Working leaves no time for just dreaming." Rafe wants never to stop working, but he hankers to explore prehistoric caves because nothing makes him feel more optimistic about human nature than 15,000-year-old cave paintings by our Cro-Magnon ancestors.

Our fantasies all seem to gather under the banner, Meet a Challenge. Or rather, Meet a New Challenge. Expanding horizons are a key ingredient, perhaps because there is a need to know we can change, affirm we can still learn as well as teach. There is a need simply to experience, to have experiences, possibly just for the sake of feeling we can.

Perhaps our dreams really march under the flag of Staying Alive. And that is best done with bracing challenges that require the cooperation of our minds. In a charming commencement address at Southampton College, writer-editor Wilfrid Sheed warned his young audience that "staying intellectually alive is very hard work. It requires willpower to stay playful, to keep your mind open. It takes character to stay alive," he said. "Only when I tried it myself did I come to realize how difficult it is to remain alive when nobody's watching and making you."

It becomes easier if you start watching other people, and noticing how they do (or don't) manage to remain alive. Beverly Sills wears a talisman engraved with the letters IDTA that stand for "I did that already." That may have helped her swap a glorious singing career for an arduous administrative one that indeed she had not done before. A forty-two-year-old magazine publisher, obsessed with conducting Mahler's *Second Symphony* although he couldn't read music, memorized the difficult ninety-minute choral symphony; he hired a professional orchestra and choir, and conducted a more than creditable performance at Lincoln Center. Moreover, several months later, the orchestra invited him to be a guest conductor.

On the other hand, I also notice people who simply wind down. Their attention turns inward, but not for daydreaming. The main action their minds get is watching a local sports team on television and/or deciding how to play a three no-trump hand. As *Newsweek* essayist Meg Greenfield wrote on awaiting her fiftieth birthday, "The important thing is not what others think about your advancing age or even what you think about it yourself—but rather what and how you think about the world outside you." Robert Penn Warren, a quarter-century older and with a poet's wisdom, said simply, "You don't wait for death; you live for death." Engagement, that's key. Exploring, stretching, expanding—the ways of engaging that keep our minds open and playful. That keep us alive.

All of us have our own songs to sing, our own What List. But I notice from those who are making the passage with particular grace that there are certain noteworthy constants to put on the How List. I'll start with optimism. After all, what but a sense that anything is still possible can account for the energy with which we throw our aging minds and bodies into new pursuits and personae? Take a publishing executive I know who, facing mandatory retirement in three years, enrolled in law school at age sixty-two. Or my eighty-two-year-old mother who recently started learning Chinese. I'm not sure whether the publisher-turning-lawyer and my mother are expressing a greater act of faith in believing that their aging minds can handle the rigors of new disciplines or that they will live long enough to make good use of them. Either way, they are invigorating their current years.

"There are very few things you can do to defy the aging process," says Dr. Stanley H. Cath, psychoanalyst, professor of psychiatry at Tufts University Medical School, and mid-life theorist. "Keeping your hopes alive is definitely one of them." Hope takes infinite forms, but one age-defying act I hadn't considered was committed by a neighbor's aunt who, half blind and almost completely deaf, bought herself a new mink coat at age eighty. "Look." She showed it to us proudly. "I'll get at least ten years' wear out of it."

Mink-clad or not, a sense of fun is definitely a requirement in the final laps. And laughter, which writer V. S. Pritchett nicely observes, "wakes up the mind." Nor will it hurt to have an ironic turn of mind that can savor life's absurd incongruities with amusement. To get a reading on this, I checked out one friend with a well-developed appetite for humor in all its manifestations. I asked what I thought was a leading question.

"What's important in the home stretch?"

"Courage," she answered unexpectedly. "So many people are consumed with anxiety. They worry and wait for terrible things to happen—all the time they're feeling fine. I don't want to have that kind of living death by anxiety." The irony was that not long after our conversation she needed that courage to face a mastectomy. "You have to dig deep," she reported, "to fight off the debilitating effect of fear."

Another friend. Another mastectomy. Same courage. Brushes with mortality seem to call up courage, or perhaps courage doesn't exist in the abstract. This friend needed radiation, then additional surgery, and will have chemotherapy the rest of her life. When I sympathetically supposed that every ache must bring renewed anxiety, she said simply, "No, I don't worry any more about every twitch. I am not going to die before I die." She remembers that she was the first of her friends to get seriously sick, and since her first operation a decade ago, seven of the then-healthy friends who visited her in the hospital are now dead. As my friend Laurie reminds me occasionally, "Aging is not for the timid."

Neither is aging for the friendless. Like many other relationships, friendship assumes new forms in mid-life. Perhaps because friendship seems more difficult to sustain these days, it becomes more precious. Friends are transferred to distant job locations. People move to new lives in new places. Couples separate, taxing our ability to hold on to each partner.

Moreover, even when friends are physically in the vicinity, they are less often available now. This is especially true of women. Women work, women study; for many of us the lunch hour is no longer a time for leisure but for errands. This hits mid-life women especially hard, because for years many of us have nurtured our friendships over noontime cottage cheese and chef salads. Now we must find substitutes: long telephone conversations; 20-minute brown bag lunches; female-only dinners that often depend on spouses being otherwise occupied. (We are the middle-aged women, remember, who are expected to dine *en famille* when other members of the *famille* want to dine.)

And as the difficulties for sustaining our friendships increase, so does the need for them. Now more than ever friendship seems essential. In mid-life we not only cherish our friends, we rely on them. And we sense that we will come to need them increasingly.

Because women can reasonably expect to outlive their spouses, they are particularly reliant on that network. "One of the critical elements in the morale of the older woman is the need for the confidante, the friend," says Dobrof. "If you watch the older students at Hunter, the ones who look better, more vibrant, are the ones who walk out arm in arm with another woman."

Lack of contact with friends is one serious complaint of mid-life women who otherwise exult in their busy working lives. Barbara, a university administrator, finds her job exhilaratingly creative—and unremittingly exhausting. We speak every couple of weeks, and she invariably sighs, "I hate not being able to spend time with my pals."

Women like Barbara make copious efforts to keep their friendships in what Samuel Johnson aptly called "a constant repair." What else could have prompted the telephone call I recently received from a friend in California I haven't seen in over ten years? She had a lot to tell about her current life. There were big changes.

Ann has a May/December marriage, and this year her husband Eric is going to be seventy. It's a number that astounds both of us. Last year, she said, Eric had a stroke. Not incapacitating but seriously disabling because Eric is an artist, and his right hand was his major tool. While Eric was learning how to use his left hand, Ann was studying to be a guidance counselor, taking her own steps toward self-reliance.

The intervening ten years evaporated as Ann reestablished contact. Suddenly I understood her call. She was assembling her network, laying in the store of support and ongoing friendship that will—does—nourish all of us. I was moved to hear from her, glad we were still interconnected.

"Hey," she said. "Don't get maudlin. I was just following instructions: 'Reach out, reach out and touch someone,' " she sang.

My hunch is that strong mid-life impulses like Ann's toward "female bonding" are rooted in Neugarten's "rehearsal for widowhood." So is learning to handle solitude, but I'm not sure those out-of-town tryouts are restricted to women. Men are not exempt from learning to be alone (if only to be self-reliant while their newly independent women are out being newly independent). If I survive Rafe, as is probable, how will I manage alone? Will I turn to a son? I'm already fishing for pledges. The scholar says I can live with him . . . as long as I remember it's *his* house. The internationalist says he'll keep in touch.

Or will I be beguiled by living alone, which, my friend Carol promises, encourages highly irregular meals, crumbs in bed, and Bogie movies, even if they begin at 3:00 A.M.? Will I start an Older Woman's Cooperative and share communal living quarters with other solitary women? Hey, they don't all have to be women. Perhaps I'll revive the old boardinghouse concept—as long as I don't have to do the cooking. Whatever form aloneness takes, all of us want to do it well. We want to cherish solitude, revel in friendships, do what we want to do, with joy. As Voltaire said, "The happiest of all lives is a busy solitude."

And if Rafe survives me, how will he manage? Does he even foresee this as a problem? A possibility?

"It won't happen," he answers firmly.

"But what would you do?" I persist.

"Move out of the house," he says. "I don't think I could live here alone . . ." His voice trails off. "I'd move to the city, have dinner with a friend, maybe teach a course. But I'm never going to retire."

There are intimations of loneliness ahead (thank goodness) but solace in change and in work, and especially in training young associates. "Besides," he grins, "women of thirty are going to pursue me." What he doesn't mention is a network of male friends; his generation of males was taught to do without it. Perhaps he doesn't forsee that he will need it. Or perhaps he really believes his playful boast.

At this half-time pause, do men and women share the same concerns for their coming years? Do middle-aged women, so lately come (if at all) to feel responsible for themselves, see independence as their prime need, while middle-aged men, according to developmental theorists, focus on their legacy? "A man's legacy is what he passes on to future generations: material possessions, creative products, enterprises, influence on others," explains Levinson. "Men differ enormously in their views about what constitutes a legacy . . . it defines to a large degree the ultimate value of his life—and his claim on immortality."

Most women are just starting to leave their own legacies of enterprise and empire; heretofore they have usually staked their claim on influence—on their children, their students, the younger generation. For parents, their separate legacies converge naturally in their offspring. Here is where each is likely to find some measure of immortality, living through children, and children's children.

My own hunch is that immortality seekers will not necessarily hit pay dirt; even the most copious planning can't ensure legacies. The road to immortality is littered with material possessions squandered, enterprises spurned, influence ignored. Our heirs may remember us, all right, but not necessarily the way we had in mind.

The key to immortality, I suspect, may lie more in keeping a light touch with future bequests and concentrating on present growth. On conducting our own lives with integrity and commitment. On standing for something.

When Rick learned of Rafe's mid-life job change, for instance, he cabled from Africa: "Don't go gentle into that good night, Pops." Cheering the stand for vitality and risk taking, he also sensed something that Rafe didn't consciously have in mind. As Rick confided to me, "Our pride, our praise, our support for Dad's proving his mettle and his integrity to you, me, and David seem almost as important to him as the actual move." He was wrong. In the long run, it was more important. As Rafe discovered, immortality can be an unexpected byproduct.

Sometimes we luck out with our dreams of immortality but more often we have to continue struggling to make sense of our mid-life condition and our dread of aging. To my surprise, our particular mid-life generation is well placed historically. Culturally, growing old is getting easier now. Given good health and adequate income (no small assumption), getting old is becoming more socially acceptable. Aging might just be in. Paradoxically, this has its roots in our youth-centered culture. We seek to remain young—or at least youthful—for so long that much of our middle years have the patina of youth: youthful activities, youthful associations, youthful zest. We have kept youthful so successfully, in fact, that we have become what Neugarten calls "an age-irrelevant society." Often our pursuits have little in common with our actual age. We see young adults in traditionally mature roles and older people in customarily youthful settings. As Neugarten remarks, "We are already familiar with the 28-year-old mayor, the 30-year-old college president, the 35-year-old grandmother, the 50-year-old retiree, the 65-year-old father of a preschooler, the 55-year-old widow who starts a business, and the 70-year-old student."

With these new and appealing trends in behavior, work, and play, the prospect of middle age is less frightening. In this supportive milieu, we look around and see that many of our colleagues are managing to have fun. "Men and women compare themselves constantly to their friends, siblings, colleagues, and parents to decide whether they are doing all right," says Neugarten. "They do not worry about being 40, 50, or 60, but about how they are doing for their age.''

Further easing our passage is a suspicion that the national reverence for youth is loosening its grip. For one thing, the demographics are in our favor. The aging and middle-aging population is increasing its ranks. There are simply more older people than ever before. Our numbers alone will provide a powerful cheering section for a more age-centered culture.

For another, we are in better health than former middle generations. All our diet and fitness obsessions are paying off in ways that may surprise us. What most of us wanted when we dove into body care was to turn the clock back. Observing our parents and other elders, we didn't expect to look, let alone feel, youthful in middle age. One fifty-eight-year-old woman voiced a common refrain, "I don't feel the way I expected to feel when I became this age."

That's the serendipitous surprise of being middle-aged—once we stop fighting it. It isn't at all what we feared. In fact, once we turn our worshipful gaze away from youth, we find we're the generation in the driver's seat. "Despite the new realization of the finiteness of time, one of the most prevailing themes expressed by middle-aged respondents is that middle adulthood is the period of maximum capacity and ability . . ." Neugarten observed from mid-life studies. "Middle-aged men and women, while they by no means regard themselves as being in command of all they survey, nevertheless recognize that they constitute the powerful age group vis-à-vis other age groups; that they are the norm bearers and the decision makers; and that they live in a society that, while it may be oriented toward youth, is controlled by the middle-aged."

The wonder is not that we are in control of much of what we survey, but that it takes us so long to find out. For so long we feel out of control, alien to our mid-life state, unable to make peace with our years, grumbling that youth is wasted on the young. Is it the human condition to feel essentially out of sync with one's age? Do we need the press of time to come to terms with our mid-life selves? Perhaps we all work best against a deadline as we try to grow up before we grow old. For myself, I know at least that when I'm even older, I don't want to look back and sigh that the middle years are wasted on the middle-aged.

In trying to make sense of the mid-life years, I am more sure of what middle age is not than of what it is. Middle age is not "45-to-65," or any other combination of numbers. Middle age is not really even a state of mind. Middle age may not exist at all. I'm coming to think that middle age is only a metaphor for a constellation of fears and dreams: fear that we are no longer young; fear that we are getting older, old; fear that time is running out and we can never realize our youthful dreams.

True, we are not exactly young. But then, we are not exactly old, either. And the nice thing about metaphors is that they can stand for several things. For instance, time-left-to-live in which to pursue our middle-aged dreams. I, for one, am starting to cultivate my afternoon garden. I am tuning in my third ear to listen for the sounds and sighs of both parents and children, gauging if I am too close, or not close enough, to the generations that bracket me. And, yes, I'm having the piano tuned, too. It looks to me as if the soil is rich and the weather is clearing to plant the seeds for some night-blooming flowers. With that familiar press of time, we may yet come of age before the coming of age.

NOTES

2   "Adults hope . . .": Daniel J. Levinson, *The Seasons of a Man's Life* (Ballantine Books, 1979), ix. Levinson is the principal author of this study of mid-life men. He was professor of psychology, Yale University School of Medicine, when the book was researched and written. His co-authors were Charlotte N. Darrow, Edward B. Klein, Maria H. Levinson, and Braxton McKee, all faculty members of the Yale Department of Psychiatry during the research.

4   "Since there are no . . .": Bernice L. Neugarten and Nancy Datan, "The Middle Years," *The Foundations of Psychiatry,* Vol. I, *American Handbook of Psychiatry,* 2nd ed. (Basic Books, 1974), 593.

5   "Among business executives . . .": Neugarten and Datan, "The Middle Years," 593.

9   "At mid-life . . .": Levinson, 215.

10   "Middle-aged people . . .": Bernice L. Neugarten, "The Awareness of Middle Age," *Middle Age and Aging: A Reader in Social Psychology* (University of Chicago Press, 1968), 94.

10   Six or seven years: Levinson, 27.

12 "For married women . . .": Neugarten, "The Awareness of Middle Age," 95.

13 "A man's fear . . .": Levinson, 214, 215.

14 "It is hard to integrate . . .": Ibid., 335.

14 Tom Wolfe, "The Generation Gap," *In Our Time* (Farrar, Straus & Giroux, 1980).

19 "One moment we act . . .": Roger L. Gould, M.D., *Transformations: Growth and Change in Adult Life* (Simon & Schuster, 1978), 223.

23 "The first . . .": Interview with Dr. Saul E. Kapel, associate professor, Cornell University Medical College.

23 All remarks by Elliott J. Rosen are from his course on family relationships sponsored by the Scarsdale Adult School.

23 "Knowing that his own death . . .": Levinson, 222.

24 "Mothers may feel . . .": Kapel interview.

24 "There are parents . . .": Ibid.

27 "involves moving out . . .": Levinson, 73.

28 "Our children can't appreciate . . .": Gould, 225.

29 "Through our children . . .": Ibid., 276.

29 "Parents too have growing pains . . .": Levinson, 255.

33 "The child who follows . . .": Gould, 190.

34 "taking them seriously . . .": Levinson, 29.

36 "It is hard for us . . .": Gould, 224.

36 "Their lives . . .": Levinson, 219.

37 "shifting the center of gravity . . .": Ibid., 57.

44 "When the children leave home . . .": Gould, 269.

44 "If we can abandon . . .": Ibid., 268.

44   "As they grow older . . .": Ibid.

45   "It can be a shock . . .": Interview with Dr. Maj-Britt Rosenbaum, Jewish-Hillside Medical Center, Long Island.

45   "There is the need . . .": Ibid.

46   "When the children leave . . .": Gould, 277.

46   "Issues of intimacy . . .": Bernice L. Neugarten, "Must Everything Be a Midlife Crisis?" *Prime Time* (February 1980), 48.

46   "Most of the themes . . .": Ibid.

47   "As we redefine ourselves . . .": Gould, 279.

48   "Often our adventures are . . .": Ibid.

52   "Ideally, in a really happy . . .": Gould, 323.

57   Noël Coward, *Private Lives* (Doubleday Doran, 1933).

61   "The prevalence of sexual stimuli . . .": Gould, 270.

61   "We feel this is our last chance . . .": Ibid., 267.

61   "If we are to understand . . .": Levinson, 258.

62   *Cosmopolitan* survey: Linda Wolfe, *The Cosmo Report* (Arbor House, 1981).

62   "The age difference . . .": Bernice L. Neugarten interviewed by Elizabeth Hall, "Acting One's Age: New Rules for Old," *Psychology Today* (April 1980), 66.

64   "so anxious about aging . . .": Levinson, 212.

65   "At mid-life a man . . .": Ibid., 253.

66   "both partners . . .": Gould, 292.

67   "Once we resolve . . .": Ibid., 215.

69   "The entry upon the psychological . . .": Elliott Jaques, "Death and the Mid-life Crisis," *International Journal of Psychoanalysis,* 46 (1965), 506.

70   "A man at mid-life is suffering . . .": Levinson, 26.

70   "many had a lifelong interest . . .": Ibid., 231.

70   "associated with manliness . . .": Ibid.

71   "Playing sports . . .": Ibid., 44.

75   "If [a man's] body . . .": Ibid., 233.

75   "Health changes . . .": Neugarten, "The Awareness of Middle Age," 96.

75   "rehearsal for widowhood": Neugarten and Datan, "The Middle Years," 599.

80   "We must risk . . .": Gould, 299.

81   "As adults . . .": Ibid., 42.

81   "that by becoming masters . . .": Gail Sheehy, *Passages: Predictable Crises of Adult Life* (Bantam Books, 1977), 404.

81   "There is the sense . . .": Rosenbaum interview.

81   "Life is restructured . . .": Neugarten and Datan, "The Middle Years," 600.

81   "The desire for stability . . .": Gould, 217.

81   "Internal voices . . .": Levinson, 200.

83   "The capacity to experience . . .": Ibid., 30.

85   "We need uncertainty . . .": Gould, 276.

86   "Men perceive a close . . .": Neugarten and Datan, "The Middle Years," 598.

87   "Many men see work . . .": Gould, 230.

87   "We pursue careers . . .": Ibid., 238.

87   "By becoming more successful . . .": Ibid., 231.

87   "If a man at 40 . . .": Levinson, 30.

87   "tentatively test . . .": Ibid., 199.

90   "Most of the women . . .": Neugarten, "The Awareness of Middle Age," 96.

90   "It's often writ . . .": Interview with Dr. Robert N. Butler, professor of geriatrics and adult development, Mount Sinai School of Medicine, New York.

91   "What a circus act . . .": Anne Morrow Lindbergh, *Gift From the Sea* (Pantheon, 1955), 26.

91   "Upon the realization . . .": Gould, 246.

92   "through definitive action.": Gould, 247.

92   "the parental imperative": David Gutmann explores the parenting stage of adult development in "Parenthood: A Key to the Comparative Study of the Life Cycle," *Life Span Developmental Psychology,* N. Datan and L. Ginsberg, eds. (Academic Press, 1975), 167–184.

92   "There appears to be . . .": Gutmann, 176.

93   "Most women . . .": Gould, 249.

93   "Husbands love less . . .": Gould, 247.

93   "A man who feels . . .": Levinson, 257.

94   "The qualities . . .": Ibid., 231.

94   "The women who . . .": Interview with Dr. Marylin R. Block, director of the National Policy Center on Women and Aging.

95   Masculine/Feminine polarity: Levinson, 228–239.

95   "Both of us are driven . . .": Gould, 278.

95   "All the male researchers . . .": Sheehy, 425.

98   "commitment is what discriminates . . .": Gould, 260.

103   "how one should relate . . .": Neugarten and Datan, "The Middle Years," 597.

103   "a thick clutter . . .": Margaret Drabble, *The Middle Ground* (Knopf, 1980), 185.

104   "concern over an aging parent . . .": Bernice L. Neugarten, "The Middle Generations," *Aging Parents* (University of Southern California Press, 1979), 259.

104   "It's fear of the burden . . .": Interview with Florence Shelley, co-author of *When Your Parents Grow Old.*

106   "The basis of our guilt . . .": Stephen DeBerry, "The Middle Aged Child and Aging Parents: A Humanistic Perspective." Paper given at a conference on aging, January 1980. All Dr. DeBerry's remarks are from this paper and conference dialogue.

106   "We are accustomed . . .": Neugarten, "The Middle Generations," 261.

106   "It is absolutely universal . . .": Interview with Dr. Rose Dobrof, director of the Brookdale Center on Aging.

107   "vestiges of unfinished business . . .": DeBerry symposium.

107   "guilt-edged insecurity," Judith Wax, *Starting in the Middle* (Holt, Rinehart & Winston, 1979).

108   "Resentment over time lost . . .": DeBerry symposium.

108   "Guilt is a two-sided . . .": Ibid.

108   "Feelings of being a burden . . .": Ibid.

109   "guilt is unavoidable . . .": Ibid.

109   "We have very few . . .": Dobrof interview.

109   "At this time . . .": Rosenbaum interview.

109   "In one way . . .": Gould, 220.

110   "Our parents hang on . . .": Ibid., 222.

112   "often the anxiety over . . .": DeBerry symposium.

115   "to sustain youthfulness . . .": Levinson, 35.

115   "the young-old": Neugarten, "Must Everything Be a Midlife Crisis?" 47.

116   "Character is extremely consistent . . .": DeBerry symposium.

118   "A number of changes . . .": Levinson, 213.

118 "a sense of the life cycle . . .": Neugarten and Datan, "The Middle Years," 604.

122 National Institute on Aging: *Special Report on Aging, 1982, Special Report on Aging, 1981, Senility, Myth or Madness?*

122 "No you should face it . . .": Rosen course.

123 "All our life . . .": Gould, 226, 228.

124 "the events are anticipated . . .": Neugarten and Datan, "The Middle Years," 605.

127 "It is as if the intensity . . .": Anne Morrow Lindbergh, *Hour of Gold, Hour of Lead* (Harcourt Brace Jovanovich, 1973).

129 "The emphasis gradually shifts . . .": Levinson, 194.

129 "We are impressed with . . .": Neugarten and Datan, "The Middle Years," 601.

129 "Between what one . . .": James Baldwin, *New York Review of Books* (March 23, 1967), 17.

130 "sometime in our forties . . .": Gould, 311.

130 Joanne Woodward interview, *The New York Times,* September 17, 1981.

131 Beverly Sills interview, *The New York Times,* September 23, 1979.

131 "Individuation . . .": Levinson, 33.

132 ego integrity: Erik H. Erikson, *Childhood and Society* (Norton, 1950), 268.

132 "On the contrary . . .": Levinson, 217.

132 "The afternoon of life": Lindbergh, *Gift From the Sea,* 86.

134 Wilfrid Sheed, commencement address at Southampton College, May 31, 1980.

134 Meg Greenfield, "On Facing Fifty," *Newsweek,* November 5, 1979.

134 Robert Penn Warren interview, *The New York Times,* June 2, 1981.

135 "There are very few things . . .": Dr. Stanley H. Cath, quoted in *The New York Times,* April 18, 1983.

135 V. S. Pritchett, "Looking Back at 80," *The New York Times,* December 14, 1980.

136 "One of the critical . . .": Dobrof interview.

138 "A man's legacy . . .": Levinson, 218.

139 "age-irrelevant": Neugarten, "Must Everything Be a Midlife Crisis?," 47.

139 "Men and women . . .": Ibid., 48.

140 "Despite the new realization . . .": Neugarten and Datan, "The Middle Years," 600.

140 "Middle-aged men and women . . .": Ibid., 596.